The In's and Out's of Online Instruction

Transitioning from Brick and Mortar to Online Teaching

Dr. Danan Myers-Wylie,
Dr. Jackie Mangieri &
Donna Hardy

Outskirts Press, Inc.
Denver, Colorado

The In's and Out's of Online Instruction
Transitioning from Brick and Mortar to Online Teaching

Outskirts Press, Inc.
http://www.outskirtspress.com

ISBN: 978-1-4327-2097-1

Library of Congress Control Number: 2008941234

Outskirts Press and the "OP" logo are trademarks belonging to Outskirts Press, Inc.

PRINTED IN THE UNITED STATES OF AMERICA

Table of Contents

Acknowledgements

There were many contributors to our book along the way. Primarily, we would like to acknowledge the patience and support of our husbands and families as we continue to strive for excellence in teaching and learning. Without their love and support, we would not be able to enjoy the work we do online today. Thank you Bob, Bob, and Marc!

We would also like to thank the instructor who brought the three of us together: Dr. Rita Marie Conrad. Dr. Conrad has been teaching, designing, and consulting about online learning for over the past decade. Through her expert facilitation, Danan, Donna, and Jackie have built a lasting friendship and business relationship. This book actually began as an assignment in one of her courses at Capella University for the Teaching Online Certification program. Rita has co-authored several books that include the Faculty Guide to Moving Teaching and Learning to the Web (2nd. Ed.) with Judith Boettcher, Engaging the Online Learner: Activities for Creative Instruction with J. Ana Donaldson, and Assessing Online Learners with Albert Oosterhof and Donald P Ely.

Another contributor to our book is Alisa Griffis, Ph.D.. Dr. Griffis was also a student at Capella University and developed a wonderful friendship and professional relationship with Danan. Dr. Griffis is the founder and president of Write Well, Write Now, Inc., a corporation dedicated to teaching scholarly, test-prep, fiction, and non-fiction writing. The website for Write Well, Write Now is: http://wwwnUSA.com. She is the author of The Power of Three: Managing Life in a Hectic World.

About the Authors

Danan Myers-Wylie, Ph.D.

Dr. Danan Myers-Wylie has a total of 22 years of teaching experience. She has taught preschool through college in both regular education and special education. She is currently an adjunct professor at Indiana Wesleyan University, American Public University Systems, and Grand Canyon University in their Masters of Education program. She also works for a Christian Online 5-12 school called Sevenstar Academy. She loves teaching online and having the flexibility of the anytime, anywhere teaching that online education offers. With this book, you too will learn the freedom that teaching online can give you.

Dr. Myers-Wylie received her Bachelors of Arts Degree from CSU-Sacramento in Child Development. She holds two teaching credentials: Multiple Subjects and Learning Handicapped. About three years ago, she decided to fulfill her lifelong goal of earning a PhD. She began taking courses online and fell in love with the format of online learning. She received a Masters in Curriculum and Instruction from University of Phoenix and graduated in 2007 with her Doctorate in Education from Capella University. Her passion for research is online instruction; specifically as it applies to orientation for learners and accommodating learners with learning handicaps.

Jacqueline Mangieri, Ph.D.

Dr. Jacqueline Mangieri has over 14 years of teaching experience at the elementary through adult level. She has taught in the traditional classroom as well as the online classroom. She is currently an adjunct professor at University of Phoenix, Grand Canyon University, Indiana Wesleyan University, and American Public University Systems. She also teaches and serves as a peer coach for the Mississippi Virtual Public School as well as Sevenstar Academy. She is excited about the possibilities for online learning to engage learners at all levels!

Dr. Mangieri received her Bachelors of Arts degree from University of MN-Morris in Elementary Education and her Master of Education degree from Bethel University in Curriculum and Instruction. She is certified K-12 with endorsements in English and Psychology. She too has been an online learner, having earned her PhD in Education from Capella University in 2008. Her passion is improving the quality of online teaching and learning for lifelong learners.

Donna Hardy

Donna Hardy has been in the education field for over seventeen years. She has worked on the academic side and is now an online faculty member. Donna comes from a strong family background in the field of teaching and has finally come back to her first love: teaching. She is currently teaching at Grand Canyon University and Indiana Wesleyan University; one in Educational Administration and the other in Business.

Donna has a Bachelors degree in Organizational Management from Northwestern College, St Paul, MN and a Masters degree in education with specializations in Online Instruction and Education Administration from Capella University, Minneapolis MN. She also holds two additional post graduate certificates from Strayer University in Marketing and Human Resources.

Future Interests

Donna and Danan, both, have a strong interest in how to prepare students and teachers for successful online transition. The In's and Out's of Online Instruction is the first in a series of books for the online instructor. Also, look for another book to help the first-time online student coming out soon.

Jackie and Danan are now working collaboratively on a book on how to differentiate instruction and learning online for all types of learners. This book will be another great How-to book to help the online instructor differentiate instruction and assignments for students who learn in different modalities as well as Gardner's multiple intelligences. It will also describe ways to work with the student with Learning Disabilities and how to best accommodate the learner's needs. Much of this book will be based on the work that they are completing for online institutions through their consulting company, The Virtual Docs: Virtual Curriculum and Instruction Associates: thevirtualdocs@gmail.com. Visit their website at www.thevirtualdocs.com.

Introduction

More and more institutions are delivering courses via the Internet. Learners who may not otherwise consider going back to school to change or better their careers are able to do so today with twenty-four/seven access to courses. Online education encourages collaborative learning, but most adult learners have been educated in a predominantly lecture-based environment. The skill of working in a collaborative environment needs to be taught.

Learning does not happen in a vacuum. It happens through interaction with our peers. Vygotsky (1981) stated that students learn from hearing the viewpoints of others. In the online classroom, students engage in discussion that allows them to express their viewpoints and hear, reflect upon, and respond to the viewpoints of others.

Piaget (1969) felt that learners must have a connection to the learning for it to be meaningful. Constructivism, defined as engaged learning, is the way one learns about the world. He further stated that acquisition of learning is more likely to occur through collaboration than alone. The online classroom engages the learner in connecting new learning to existing life experiences. The learners are encouraged to engage in discussions with classmates that will express different points of view on the same subject. As peers, the learners discuss and question each other's points of view.

Problem-based learning was a major step towards collaborative learning. In problem-based learning, learners work together in teams to define the problem and come to a solution. The process of problem-based learning applies directly to the learner's career and leads to lifelong learning. Online learning opportunities provide a natural opportunity for learners to engage collaboratively in problem-based learning.

Online learning communities are a group of diverse individuals with skills and training of varying levels, knowledge, experiences, and expertise interacting in a collaborative environment with the use of technological tools and resources. The online learning community aim to provide students with greater curricular coherence. They provide the students and instructor an opportunity for increased intellectual interaction and shared inquiry.

This book will assist faculty members to determine if online teaching is a good fit and, if it is, to find a position and make the transition from the brick-and-mortar classroom to online instruction. This book will also help the new online instructor become more comfortable and efficient in the classroom. You will find ideas and suggestions for setting up and maintaining a positive, inviting online classroom that invites collaboration from your students. Tips and shortcuts for managing your online class, including grading all aspects of the online classroom, will be offered. Finally, strategies for handling challenges that accompany online learning, such as plagiarism and difficult students, will be explored.

Chapter One

Things to Consider

Thank you so much for all of your patience and care over the duration of this course. I learned a great deal throughout the four workshops and appreciate the opportunity to show some of that in the Workshop 4 materials. I want to thank you again for e-mailing me and even calling me (I received the voicemail after I had read the e-mail) if it wasn't for your effort that went above and beyond anything I could have asked for, I would definitely be facing even greater challenges.

Thanks again,
Jason

Online teaching is rewarding and exciting. It enables educators to work from home or anywhere in the world where there is an Internet connection. It is flexible and allows instructors to teach early in the morning, in the middle of the day, and/or late at night if they wish. With online instruction growing at a more rapid pace than traditional brick-and-mortar classroom instruction, a classroom instructor or college professor who is considering making the switch to online instruction has many things to think about before making the leap.

The Basics

Just like learning online, teaching online is not for everyone. First, there is a particular skill-set that the potential online instructor must engender in order to be successful and efficient in the online environment. Rapid and proficient typing skills are necessary. Although universities hiring online instructors do not test typing speeds, in order to make the most efficient use of one's time, but having good typing skills are essential.

Next, the online instructor must have flawless grammar, punctuation, and sentence structure. Since virtually all communication is conducted solely via writing, the online instructor must be able to compose swiftly and be extremely accurate as a proofreader of one's own work. The online instructor must be committed to logging in daily (at least six days each week) and sometimes several times a day to both e-mail and to the online classroom. Finally, a successful online educator develops a warm and approachable virtual classroom presence, which – considering the students cannot see nor hear the instructor – is more difficult to develop than the in-person classroom. Fortunately, it is possible to learn the methodologies in creating warmth and a winning tone in the online classroom.

Before making the move to online teaching, you must consider how this will affect your finances and budget. Full-time positions, complete with benefits, are rare and hard to come by. Most institutions prefer to use adjunct faculty to fill online positions. This means your teaching contracts are sporadic and at-will; being offered a contract one term does not guarantee you will be offered another the next term. Paychecks will not necessarily arrive predictably on the first and 15th of the month. During busy months, online faculty members must be disciplined to save some of their income for other months when contracts are not as plentiful.

One drawback to being an adjunct or part-time employee is the lack of benefits. If you are going to work online full-time, you will need to make sure you have your own health insurance, life insurance, and retirement plan. Some universities even hire you as a contract employee where you will need to make sure that you pay your taxes and social security benefits. It is a good idea to hire a financial planner or tax professional to advise you as you make wise financial decisions.

Self-motivation

Teaching online requires self-motivation. Since you work at home, it is so easy to get distracted with other activities such as chores, shopping, visiting with friends, and so on. You do set your own schedule, which is one of the benefits. However, most universities would like you to log on and participate at least four to five times per week; many online instructors find they feel "behind" if they do not check in at least once per day. You have papers to grade, discussions to monitor, and sometimes journals to read. There are questions to answer. All of this takes time.

Because teaching online is in fact a job, it must be treated as such. You would do well to schedule your day just as you might if you were teaching classes on campus. Some universities require you to hold specific "office hours" when you are available to students via phone or online for immediate response, but even if this is not required, you may wish to schedule such hours and publicize these to your students. While it is great to have the flexibility mentioned above, you do have a responsibility to your online students and you must schedule your days accordingly.

Still, teaching online gives you the freedom of where you teach. The authors have taught while on vacation in Japan, Hawaii, Mexico, the Bahamas, and on cruises. We take our laptops and visit family. We even spend four months a year at a lake cabin or boating and still teach. Therefore, you really can enjoy your life and still earn an income - any time, anywhere!

Self-Check

This checklist can help you to determine of you are a good "fit" for online teaching. You should have a majority of the following characteristics:

1. Good time management
2. Well organized with space and course materials
3. Strong subject matter knowledge
4. Plans ahead

5. Understands basic computer knowledge
6. Can organize the computer with files and folders
7. Your computer has at least at least 250k+ram, 1ghz or faster processor, 60-80 gigabyte hard drive, etc.
8. Have installed ms office suite, internet explorer, realplayer, winzip, and shockwave
9. Working knowledge of ms office suite, internet explorer, realplayer, winzip, and shockwave
10. Must possess a high speed internet connection
11. Knowledge of web surfing, how to use search engines by expanding or narrowing a search using boolean advanced search techniques
12. Know how to download a file from the internet
13. Know how to attach documents to an outgoing email
14. Can give step by step instructions on how to use the internet or computer to a student in writing
15. Communicates well in writing -articulates thoughts and expressions in clear, concise writing
16. Attention to detail
17. Excellent typing skills
18. Can convey personality and/or emotions through writing
19. Can use email efficiently and effectively
20. Knowledge of and uses "bookmarks" or "favorites" for internet pages.
21. Good understanding of netiquette, academic honesty, and APA style formatting
22. Uses internet resources in instruction

So, did you discover that you do not possess a majority of these characteristics? Do not give up! Keep reading. You will learn many of these characteristics throughout this book.

Chapter Two

How To Get An Online Position

I assumed all facilitators would be like you. Wrong!

Lora Jean

It takes dedication and time to find just the right program that fits your experience and education, and it can take even more dedication and time then to be hired. Many universities and K-12 institutions are offering online courses today. Some are looking for instructors to teach a blend of online and traditional courses. Advertisements for these types of positions will say something like "daily/weekly presence on campus is required." Most universities hiring online instructors do not have full time positions available; most are adjunct or part-time and the online instructor may only teach 5 – 6 classes per year. This provides a nice "additional" income to a full time teaching position, but does not provide enough income to work solely from home. This issue adds the additional burden of finding more than one adjunct position at more than one university or other educational institution. Although there is a wide variety in hiring processes, often a training class, and/or mentoring experience is part of the hiring process. It can take from a minimum of a few weeks or months to several years to be hired for an online position. Perseverance is the key!

Finding that perfect position

How do you find that perfect position? There are several online resources that can help you with your job search. The Peterson's Guide to Distance Learning Programs (http://www.petersons.com/distancelearning/) will guide you to several possible matches for your area of expertise. Other websites such as higheredjobs.com, chronicle.com/jobs, adjunctnation.com, and adjunctadvocate.com have job boards where you can search for positions. There are also several online discussion groups where current and prospective online faculty network and share leads; Yahoo! groups have more than one group for online adjuncts where networking occurs and job opportunities are passed along.

You can also use the more traditional methodology of going to your library. There are books that list all of the universities. Some list them by degree. Copy the pages to all of the universities that have programs in your area of expertise. Then visit their websites. See if there are job openings. Even apply if there are not. You never know when an opening will pop up and your name is already there. This has happened more than once to the authors.

A great way to find a position is networking – actually knowing someone who can personally recommend you for a position. Perhaps you have heard a colleague or friend talk about a great adjunct job that they love. Talk to the person and learn more about the job and the university. Ask about openings. Most importantly, ask if you can use them as a reference.

10 Tips for Resume/Curriculum Vitae Writing

1. Use titles or headings that match the teaching positions you are looking for
2. Use a design that grabs attention
3. Create content that sells you as an instructor
4. Quantify and use power words
5. Use key words from the advertisement for the position you are applying
6. Look for hidden needs of the employer
7. Sell yourself and your skills
8. Create an image that matches the salary you want
9. Prioritize the content of your resume/vitae to match the position in which you are applying

10. Address the specific skills that the employer is looking for in your resume/vitae and cover letter

Applying for positions

As you fill out and send applications, keep a list or spreadsheet of all of the institutions and positions for which you apply. A motivated instructor may apply at several universities for various positions. Therefore, it is important to know which universities and positions you have applied to in order to actively pursue them.

One key is to always check back. Once your application and vitae have been received, you will likely receive an acknowledgement via email. Save this email that states your application has been received and forwarded to the proper department. This is your connection in checking back on your application.

Often universities advertise to gather a "hiring pool". There is not necessarily a position available. Alternatively, you may find that positions you are applying for are six to nine months out. The application goes through the human resource department, who is your initial contact, and is then forwarded on to the dean of the university or appropriate academic department. It sits in a pile of information for the dean to read. Alternatively, the secretary has filed it away in a "hiring pool" file and the application has not even been glanced over.

Bring your name to the forefront of human resources. About two weeks after the application is received, send a response back to the email asking about the process. Most often, human resources will do one of two things. They will either find out where the application is in the process and let your know, or, e-mail the name and e-mail address of the dean and department for which you applied. Now your foot is in the door. E-mail the dean and let him/her know your interest. Let the dean see your name. When a job comes available, that name is going to come to mind.

Another way to make you name known to the dean is to ask if there are any curriculum development projects that need to be completed. Often there are little projects that need to be completed that are not being addressed by anyone. These can be given to you to complete for a small stipend. Even volunteering for little jobs such as rewording a rubric or assignment helps to give you priority for the next teaching assignments. I cannot tell you how many extra assignments and small contracts I have received from using this approach.

Interviews

Different universities interview differently. In the authors' experience, an interview has two parts: preliminary and formal. Usually the preliminary interview is an email asking a set of questions about how you work with students and your experience both as an online instructor and as a content expert. Some sample questions for this preliminary interview include the following:

- What do you know about the university?
- How did you hear about the opening?
- What specifically interests you about becoming an online instructor?
- Why do you think you will be successful?
- When instructors have a passion for teaching, it shows in the classroom. How would you create a positive learner-centered environment?
- In what general subject area(s) are you interested in teaching?
- If you are asked to teach a course that you have never taught before, what will you do to prepare yourself?
- What methods would you implement to aid in your students' education?
- How will you handle difficult students?

Sometimes a university may send you a paper and ask you to correct it. The university wants to see how well versed the candidates are in APA format. It is important when grading to show a balance between constructive criticism and positive comments. Be careful to pay close attention to the appropriate ways to cite sources and write references. The university also wants to know that the candidate has strong grammatical skills, beyond what Microsoft Word is going to find in the editing process.

After the preliminary interview, a formal time will be set for a phone interview. There are two things to do to prepare for this interview. The first is to learn everything you can about the university. Create notes that you can refer to during the interview that include answers to the following questions:

- What is the history of the university?
- What is the university's philosophy?
- What is the Mission statement?
- Who is the clientele?
- What are the levels of education?
- What degrees are offered?
- What courses are you a content expert?

The second step is to schedule this interview at a time and place when you will not be distracted. Send the children to the neighbors or to the movies with your spouse or a friend. Have a cup of tea or hot chocolate to calm your nerves. Make sure you have the university uploaded on your browser and your notes nearby. You are now ready for your interview!

Training

Most online universities have a training program to teach you their philosophy and their expectations for working with the students. These trainings can be anywhere between two and five weeks long. You are not paid during this time but it is probably the most important part of the hiring process. The authors have been through trainings at many different universities. Each one is different so it is important to put your best foot forward. This is the time that the university is looking at you to see how often you are available, how active you are in the class, how well you communicate, and how well you know the university. Prior to your training, review the information about the university. This will help you know the proper way to respond to the assignments.

While in the training, be prepared to visit the training room twice a day every day. Course rooms have a place that the instructor can view when you log on and track your activity. Here are some tips for making a great impression in the training class:

- Make sure that you read everything before beginning any of the activities.
- Print out the material and place it in a binder for easy access. Most of what you will learn will be the university's expectations for working in the classroom and how to set up your classroom and you will need to refer to this information once you have your first course.
- Respond to discussion questions early in the week.
- Respond to the other colleagues often. If there is a minimum expectation, do more than the minimum.
- Finish all assignments early in the week.
- Make sure you fully understand what is expected for each assignment.
- Ask questions.
- Help your colleagues by answering their questions if you know the answers.
- Take time to learn the in's and out's of the course room.

Chapter Three

Organization

Danan has a wonderful rapport with her online students. Her ability to connect with her students and talent for teaching in the online format makes for a successful online learning experience.

She sets up "office hours" and is there; answers course related and university protocol questions, as well as technology questions and just about any questions; is ever present in the weekly dialogs encouraging students with knowledgeable comments or leading questions; reads weekly assignments and provides pertinent, detailed feedback. When one is out there in cyberspace, it is good to have someone like Danan to help navigate the unknown.

Barbara

Organization in any career is important. It is equally or more important to be organized for your online courses. In fact, if you just jump right in without giving some thought to the issues of organizing your time and your space, you will find that your job is much more stressful and time consuming than it needs to be.

Organizing your time

It is so easy to spend far too much time on the computer. Online instruction is a job, not a life style. Keeping a balance between your personal life and teaching is very important and not easy. The goal of effective time management is to know how you spend your time and make purposeful decisions on how to balance work, family, and leisure time. To learn good time management skills, you must be dedicated and want to change your habits.

It is extremely important to begin with an organizational system in place. Think about the traditional brick and mortar university. There are set start and end times. Classes are slotted into segments within the day and week. The classroom doors are closed on weekends and holidays.

It could not be more different in the virtual world! In the online classroom, the biggest draw for both students and instructors is the anytime, anywhere aspect. Students and instructors can work any hour of the day or night, any day of the week, any time of the year. Many online instructors enjoy this flexibility, but it can also present challenges of spending too much time in front of the computer screen. The solution is to create a schedule! It is very important for you to define when you are working and when you are not.

Take some time to create a tentative work schedule for yourself. Begin by monitoring how much time you use each week for the following activities: sleeping, eating, driving to and from work – that is if you work out of the home, leisure activities, chores, work – besides your work online, family activities, and exercise. Calculate the amount of time you will have or need each week for teaching your classes. Use a daily planner as a tool for managing your time efficiently. Then create an hour-by-hour schedule for the week, building a routine that includes time for everything in your life. Make sure to schedule in breaks. If you work just at home, make sure to take coffee breaks and a lunch away from your computer. It is okay if you find it takes some time to find the right routine for you and your family, but it is critical to find and maintain the right balance. It is vitally important to keep a good balance in your life that includes time for exercise, relaxation, sleep, and meals as well as quality time for family, friends, and community events.

Teaching online, no matter what you think, is not easier than teaching in a brick and mortar university. Yes, the commute is great but still, one must be realistic. Expect to spend at least as much time in an online course as you would in a traditional classroom. Schedule your class time weekly, just as if you were going to the university to teach. Usually classes are 3 to 4 hours in length per week. Schedule this amount of time for "attending" class. You should also schedule the same amount of time for grading papers and answering student questions. The best part with online courses is this time is flexible. It does not need to be done all at once.

At one time, the author had three universities, teaching a total of five classes. Keep in mind that five classes would be a total of 40 hours a week of class time. Only 36 hours are necessary if you are well organized, trimming a minimum of 4 hours per week. This leaves plenty of time and flexible to take care of family, personal, and spiritual needs.

Sunday: *Day off.*

Monday: *Two hours grading. Two hours participating in discussions and answering questions. Two hours preparing and setting up material for classes.*

Tuesday: *Four hours grading papers. Two hours participating in discussions and answering questions.*

Wednesday: *Four hours grading papers. Two hours participating in discussions and answering questions.*

Thursday: *Four hours grading papers. Two hours participating in discussions and answering questions.*

Friday: *Four hours grading papers. Two hours participating in discussions and answering questions.*

Saturday: *Two hours preparing and setting up material for classes. Two hours participating in discussions and answering questions.*

Organizing your workspace

It is equally important to organize your workspace. Many online instructors work at home for part or all of the day. The majority of work in an online class is completed at the computer. Therefore, it is important to think about the ergonomics of your workspace at home.

Ideally, you already have an office area where you can work comfortably. A good chair is imperative. The chair needs to give good support for back and shoulders. Equally important is having a desk at the correct height for proper resting of the hands and arms. A good ergonomic keyboard may be necessary to keep from getting tendonitis or carpal tunnel. When course writing and grading is heavy, the use of voice recognition software can also be helpful.

Keep clutter to a minimum and have within reach all materials needed for your courses. These materials would include training manuals for the school, as well as books and other course materials. You also want easy access to phone numbers, emails, and addresses. Keeping all of your materials organized saves time from hunting through piles of material to find a specific paper.

Organizing your computer

The most important organization is of your computer itself. Folders, just like in a traditional brick and mortar setting, are important. Have a folder for each university and each course you teach. You may even want to divide a course folder into weekly information, to allow for easy access and uploading of materials. Keep grading rubrics in a file. Label them by assignment and week. For example, the Literature Review assignment should have a rubric labeled "Literature Review Rubric – week 2". This same labeling should be used for sample papers and templates.

Finally, the most important part, back up your files on an external hard drive, thumb drive, or disc. The creation of materials is time consuming. Technology is fragile. A virus on your system or hard drive crash could destroy all of your files, which could necessitate the recreation of everything you use. Do not think this will not happen to you. It is much better to be safe than sorry.

Chapter Four

Building a Positive Environment

Above all things, Danan has never forgotten that we are human beings. With online courses, it is too easy to forget that there are actual people behind these responses and submitting our weekly assignments. She takes the time to remember that we are separate individuals when assisting with assignments and providing feedback. Students enroll in online courses because of overwhelmingly busy work and family schedules and Danan seems to always remember that fact.

Alejandra

When teaching at any level, caring has to be evident to the students in everything an instructor does. Building a safe environment where the students feel comfortable taking risks and sharing about their personal lives is the most important part of managing the online classroom. In teaching, you become a mentor, role model, and someone your students can depend upon and trust.

Online instructors should demonstrate a positive attitude, be enthusiastic about learning, exhibit critical thinking skills, and show compassion for others. Since the authors have all been online students, we want the students to know that we have walked in their steps and we understand the frustrations, and concern that they may have. Therefore, as an instructor we need to not only build a safe environment, but also exhibit flexibility and continue to be a life-long learner.

Roles of the Learner and Instructor

The role of an engaged learner develops over time. In the fast-pace of online learning, the online learner must quickly become comfortable with technology and using text-based communication, and they most demonstrate a higher level of self-directed learning than they would need in a traditional classroom. Becoming comfortable with all of the above is crucial to becoming a successful online learner (Palloff & Pratt, 2003).

The instructor of the online classroom can help the learners become comfortable in the online classroom, whether it is their first course or one of many. Online learning today is often a social and collaborative endeavor, with mandated participation in discussion or assignments with other classmates often a required component of the course of study. The goal of the instructor is to stimulate the learners to actively participate in the learning situation; thus enabling the learner to gain the most knowledge from being a member of the online community and to share their knowledge and experiences with their learning peers. According to Conrad and Donaldson (2004), the learner goes through four phases of engagement as explained below. Depending on which phase a student is in, the collaboration will be different. Therefore, the role of the instructor will change.

Phase One

In phase one, the learner is a newcomer. Because of this, the instructor is a "social negotiator" (Conrad and Donaldson, 2004). During this phase, the instructor provides activities to help learners get to know each other such as student biographies. The expectations for the course, including participation, are posted for students to read, acknowledge, and ask clarifying questions.

During Phase One, which typically spans the first couple of weeks of the course, the instructor must be highly involved in the discussions. Each student posting and response should be read to make sure that students are working up to course expectations and any questions or concerns are promptly acknowledged and addressed. This assures the new students that the instructor is in fact a real person who will be involved in the learning process and cares about their success in the class.

When dealing with brand-new online students, the importance of answering student questions and concerns as quickly as possible cannot be understated. This means that the instructor needs to be available many times throughout the day for the first two weeks as opposed to later in the course when the instructor may only check in once per day and only five or six days per week. As students begin to post, it helps to send them a private e-mail to tell them they are on target and doing a good job. Students appreciate this validation as it helps them to feel comfortable and assured, without a stifling and dominating instructor presence in the actual discussion forums.

There is a fine balance in responding to students' discussion posts. Yes, it is important for the students to get feedback as soon as possible. However, responding too soon or to often can stifle a discussion as students start to wait and rely on the instructor for responses instead of responding to one another. Wait to respond to anyone until after the first few students have posted the initial response to the question. In the first couple of weeks, try to respond to each student one time, whether it is to an initial post to the discussion question or within a discussion thread. Charting the names of the students and actually tracking when and how often you respond to them is helpful to make sure you do not miss any students or do not respond to some students in disproportionate manner.

Phase Two

During the second phase, the learner's role is one of cooperator. The instructor is the "structural engineer" (Conrad and Donaldson, 2004). The students have had some time to get to know each other and learn how to navigate through the classroom. Now is the time to form small groups and provide activities that require critical thinking, reflection, and the sharing of ideas. The instructor should still be visible in the classroom but the amount of postings can drop down to two or three per day. Of course, the instructor must continue to respond to student questions quickly. However, it is critical that the instructor has a visible presence in the content discussion as well.

Phase Three

The learner becomes the collaborator in phase three. The instructor is the facilitator and can take a step back in guiding the discussions. This does not mean, "Do not participate". However, responding to one or two students a day is usually enough to keep discussions lively. Activities may be provided that require small groups to collaborate, solve problems, and reflect on experiences. The students have had time to get to know each other and share ideas. They are ready to begin collaborating on projects.

Phase Four

Phase four is the final phase where students become initiators or partners in the classroom. Discussions begin to go not only where the instructor intends but also where the learners direct them to go and the instructor should welcome this as an exciting development! At this time, the instructor's role becomes more equal as part of the learning community. The instructor becomes the challenger to bring out higher levels of critical thinking within the discussions and group interaction. Activities are learner-designed or learner-led (Conrad & Donaldson, 2004).

Lesson clarity

Often times the assignments that are written for the students are vague or confusing. It is vitally important that the online instructor is an expert on the topic so more details can be added to clarify the assignment. In looking at an assignment, the writers check to make sure that all assignments are easily understood by using the following guidelines:

1. Make sure all directions are detailed.
2. Simplify explanations of assignments. Give step-by-step directions.
3. Use appropriate examples/experience to model assignment expectations.
4. Emphasize, repeat, and elaborate difficult and important points.
5. Clearly define unfamiliar/difficult terms.
6. Provide templates for large or difficult assignments.
7. Do not over rely on samples assignments as you may receive clones.

Here is an example of an assignment given to students who are in a Master's in Education class where the students are all classroom instructors:

Culture Chart

Design a chart to compare and contrast the characteristics of 4-5 different cultural group norms and values. Include age, gender, language, and social values. Describe how these factors influence learning.

The assignment can then be broken down as follows:

*Design a chart to compare and contrast the characteristics of 4-5 different cultural group norms and values that you find in your school or community. This can be but is not limited to Hispanic, Arabic, Russian, East Indian, Native Americans, and African Americans. Include **age of adulthood, gender differences such as matriarch or patriarch society, home language, and social values**. Then**, in an essay, describe how these factors influence learning**. I have provided a template for you to use to complete this assignment. Make sure that you are using APA format for your paper.*

This can be a challenging assignment. Finding the information on the Internet may be a bit frustrating, but you can do it! ☺ You will need to do some footwork. Use your resources at your school and district. Ask the bilingual paraprofessionals, your English Language Resource Instructor, older students, parents, your outreach consultants or school counselors.

Interesting/engaging lessons

Courses at most universities are written by professional curriculum writers. All of the courses are written in the same format, giving cohesiveness to the program and universities do not want you to deviate from this material due to accreditation concerns. Universities need to be able to assure accrediting bodies of the rigor of their programs, and this is one step they have taken when students and faculty members are geographically dispersed. While faculty may have some flexibility for some assignments, other required components of some programs (such as electronic portfolios) must be delivered exactly as written, so instructors must be familiar with the policies and guidelines set forth by their institution's administration. Also, faculty members may have an opportunity for involvement in such curriculum development opportunities as institutions must also show accrediting bodies that faculty have an active role in this development, so if interested, faculty members should express their interest in this role.

Universities have set policies for changing or adding course material. Make sure that you know the process for receiving permission to make changes or add. If it is possible to present the material in different formats, make sure to keep the presentation short and keep it aligned with the course goals, objectives, and material.

Most courses are written in text format. A weekly module includes the lecture as well as the assignments. This is format is great for the visual learner. However, we cannot assume that all of our students will be visual learners. On top of that, students begin to skim lectures and assignments, thus missing important details.

There will be some universities that you will need to write your own material from syllabus to each individual assignment. Here are the guidelines used in presenting material in the online classroom:

1. Present material in a variety of formats. Use presentations, charts, graphs, video, podcasts, blogs, wikis, etc. in addition to printed lectures and other text-based course materials.
2. If allowed, give the students choices in completing assignments. Students get tired of writing paper after paper each week, and faculty also get tired of grading paper after paper each week!
3. Refer to your own life or professional experience. You have been hired for your expertise, and students enjoy hearing from you about how course theory translates into practical application.

An exemplary online instructor will vary the format of presentation. It is very easy to take the lecture notes and create a Power-Point presentation for students to view. Often presentations will help the kinesthetic learner if they are interactive. To help your auditory learners, try adding a voice clip to the presentation. Most current computers include sound recording software to make voice recording very easy. You can also download Audacity (http://audacity.sourceforge.net/), an open-source software for recording and editing sounds and audio; be sure to also download the LAME encoder so your computer can read the file as an mp3 file.

One way to really help the students, if you have some academic freedom, you may need to get college approval beforehand, is to vary the way assignments are completed. The straight APA formatted paper gets to be redundant for both the student and instructor. Spice it up! Look through the assignments and see what other ways the information can be presented. For example, a compare and contrast assignment can be shown in a Venn diagram with a summary following. Some assignments would make good presentations or brochures that the student can later use in their career. Again, being a subject area expert and knowing your material really helps in how you can alter the assignment.

Chapter Five

Welcome Students to the Class

One simple but effective element that Danan adds as an online instructor is the heading "Ask Danan" on our discussion page. This welcomes our questions for clarity about assigments, gives specific and immediate feedback, and allows participants to feel more relaxed rather than frustrated. Her answers are warm, encouraging, and to the point. When she is willing to dialogue with each individual, we know there is a caring person behind the instructor's role.

Lora Jean

Setting the stage

Setting the stage is very important. Some universities give you the ability to contact your students before the class begins. Others do not give access until the day the course begins. Either way, a welcome email is an awesome way to set the stage for your classroom. It adds a personal touch that often invites the most intimidated learner into the classroom.

This welcome email should be brief. Remember, it is an invitation to come to class. It should not have extra information about procedures and routines. Some things to include in this invitation to your course are information on how to access the classroom, your personal information, and how to be successful in your class.

Hi,

Welcome to your online course! My name is Dr. Danan Myers-Wylie and I will be your instructor for this course. Please call me Danan. I have been involved in online education since 2002 and have worked in education for over twenty-one years. My detailed introduction is in the Cybercafé.

Online learning can be challenging, yet rewarding. In my experience, I learn more by being involved in the discussions than I would in a traditional classroom. Online learning is fast-paced. It is very important that you read everything because the three reasons students lose points or receive lower grades are lack of reading; lack of understanding and not asking clarifying questions; and lack of editing or rereading for grammar, spelling, and APA.

Each week you will find the "expectations" for the week. This is the most important document to read. It is your "road map" for the week's activities. I have also enclosed a course calendar. Print it out and post near your computer. Cross off each assignment as you complete it. This will help you keep track of your assignments and also give you a sense of accomplishment. If you have any questions, please do not hesitate to ask.

Along with this calendar, post my email and phone number somewhere you can easily access it off your computer. I used to keep my professor's information in my briefcase so I had it with me no matter where I went. Here is my email and phone number:

I look forward to seeing you in class. To access your course, go to www.accesscourse.edu. Type in your user name and password. You will find a link to our classroom there. I look forward to seeing you inside!

Danan

Provide a calendar

It is very easy to make a calendar for the course. Make sure that your calendar is not set up beginning on Sunday if your course begins on a different day of the week. In the example shown below, courses begin on Thursday and end on Wednesday, so the calendar is set up to show the first day of the week as Thursday.

When sending out the calendar to the students, it is nice to color code the assignments. For example, everything to do with discussions can be blue, individual assignments are red, and group assignments are green. This helps them to visually differentiate between the types of assignments. The following pages contain a sample course calendar.

Course Calendar – Week 1 & 2

Thur	Fri	Sat	Sun	Mon	Tues	Wed
5	6	7	8	9	10	11
1st day of class	Complete bio in cyber-café	Post initial responses to week 1 discussion questions			Respond to 3 peers' week 1 discussion questions	History of Sp. Ed. Law Paper Due
Week 1 begins						
Read ch. 1 and websites						

Thur	Fri	Sat	Sun	Mon	Tues	Wed
12	13	14	15	16	17	18
Week 2 begins	Week 1 Journal Due	Post initial responses to week 2 discussion questions			Respond to 3 peers' week 2 discussion questions	Least Restrictive Environment Paper Due
Read ch. 2 and websites						
Give Danan requests for group assignments'						

Course Calendar – Week 3 & 4

Thur	Fri	Sat	Sun	Mon	Tues	Wed
19	20	21	22	23	24	25
Week 3 begins	Week 2 Journal Due	Post initial responses to week 3 discussion questions			Respond to 3 peers' week 3 discussion questions	Group Assignment – IEPs Paper Due
Read ch. 4 and websites			29	30	31	1
26	27	28				
Week 4 begins	Week 3 Journal Due	Post initial responses to week 4 discussion questions			Respond to 3 peers' week 4 discussion questions	Adequate Progress Paper Due
Read ch. 2 and websites						

Course Calendar – Week 5 & 6

Thur	Fri	Sat	Sun	Mon	Tues	Wed
2	3	4	5	6	7	8
Week 5 begins	Week 4 Journal Due	Post initial responses to week 5 discussion questions			Respond to 3 peers' week 5 discussion questions	Due Process and Parental Rights Paper Due
Read ch. 4 and websites						
9	10	11	12	13	14	15
Week 6 begins	Week 5 Journal Due	Post initial responses to week 6 discussion questions			Respond to 3 peers' week 6 discussion questions	CLC – Supplemental Services Paper Due
Read ch. 6 and websites						

Course Calendar – Week 7 & 8

Thur	Fri	Sat	Sun	Mon	Tues	Wed
16	17	18	19	20	21	22
Week 7 begins	Week 6 Journal Due	Post initial responses to week 7 discussion questions			Respond to 3 peers' week 7 discussion questions	Discipline Paper Due
Read ch. 5 and websites						
23	24	25	26	27	28	1
Week 8 begins	Week 7 Journal Due	Post initial responses to week 8 discussion questions			Respond to 3 peers' week 8 discussion questions	Last day of class
Read ch. 6 and websites						Week 8 Journal due
						Dispute Resolutions Paper Due
						All work due

Send an e-card

A really nice touch above and beyond a welcome email, is to send the students an e-card. An e-card is just like a regular paper card, except it is sent via email. You can send an e-card to welcome students to class, or you can send one to commemorate something they have shared in class, such as the birth of a child, a job promotion, death of a family member, or other event. There are many sites that offer free cards. No registration is needed. Remember, companies that offer free services will often try to offer you services for a price so be wary when sharing your personal information. Check to see if there are any boxes checked about receiving free information or sharing of your personal information and uncheck them before sending your e-card. The following sites have great cards to send to students and offer a nice selection of everyday cards to choose from:

1. Bluemountain http://www.bluemountain.com/
2. E-Cards http://www.e-cards.com/
3. 123 Cards http://www.123greetings.com/
4. Web Cards http://www.webwinds.com/cards/cards.htm

Classroom climate

Classroom climate is extremely important. This begins with your welcome to the students and continues through all of your communication and expectations of student behavior.

1. Provide timely, encouraging feedback
2. Be approachable.
3. Give guidelines for discussions and interaction between classmates.

Feedback is very important. Most universities give instructors between 48 hours and seven days to provide the student feedback on written assignments. It is extremely important to provide feedback as soon as possible. With an eight-week course that has assignments due each week, feedback must be provided quickly enough to allow the student to use the instructor's comments and suggestions in the writing of their next paper. If the instructor takes the full week to give feedback, the students continue to make the same errors. More on feedback will be given in another chapter.

Instructors need to be approachable. In the online environment, it is vital to make sure that your words are welcoming and show compassion for the students. This begins at the beginning of the class with the welcome to the students.

Sample Welcome Letter 1

Welcome to the class! My name is Danan Myers-Wylie. Please call me Danan. I will be your instructor for this class. I have been in education for a little over 21 years and have taught preschool through adults in both regular education and special education settings.

My office hours are early AM and evening, central time. At that time, I will check for any questions that you may have posted. You may also email me at d.myerswylie@email.net or call (123)456-7890 (cell). Please make sure you leave a message.

My goal for this class is to help you be successful. The reason most students do not do well online is that they do not read or follow the directions. If there is something you do not understand, please ask for clarification.

Not too long ago, 2002, I was a first time online learner. Choosing to learn online sounded so easy. For a person who used a computer to print out fill-in-the-blank pages for her students, I had a lot to learn! For example, how do you attach papers, surf the Net, access Course rooms, use a chat room. I had no idea it was going to be so hard. That is why I am here

31

to help you be successful. I made it through both my Master's and Doctorate and you will make your dreams come true too!

Sample Welcome Letter 2

My name is Donna Hardy and I will be your instructor and your partner in learning for this class. Please feel free to call me Donna. I have been involved in online education since 2000 and have worked in education for seventeen years.

My online office hours are 7:00 p.m. to 9:00 p.m. CDT, Monday - Friday. My preferred way of communication is via email. My email is dhardy@email.net and my telephone number (cell) is (123)456-7890.

Sometimes you may need to talk to me directly. To schedule a phone conference, please email me with a few times that will work for you and I will get back to you with a time within 24 hours.

For your first day in the classroom, please take some time to get to know your classroom. Spend some time navigating through the links on the left. Read the syllabus. Then visit the "Cybercafé" through the "Discussion" link. There you will find my personal biography. Please take the time to read my bio and post one of your own. During this first week, we will take time to get to know each other through our biographies and responding to each other's bios and discussion questions.

I remember only too well how I felt in my first online course. Totally overwhelmed! I was so thankful to have instructors and advisors who cared to take the time to help me and answer all my 'questions' which were numerous. That is what I want to do for you. Please ask all the questions you have. I want to help you make your goals become a reality.

After the welcome letter, it is important to be noticeable in the classroom. Post a separate section for questions. Make sure to answer questions as soon as possible.

One area that students really appreciate is knowing that you care about them as individuals. Many instructors are very strict about deadlines and late assignments. As an online learner, I had a family emergency. I will never forget the compassion of one instructor who reached out to me. She asked if I would need any extra time to complete assignments. Then she stayed in touch to see how I was even after the class. I knew that I wanted to show this type of compassion to my students.

I understand that life happens. We all have jobs, families, and other obligations outside of school. These obligations may get in the way of your schooling. If you have a family emergency or event, extra load at work, or another obligation and will need extra time, please do not hesitate to ask. I truly understand that we need to go with the flow of what life gives us.

With that said, one of the beautiful things about online education is the ability to work in advance. You have access to all of the course materials, so if you know that you are going to be heading into a busy time of your life, be sure to plan ahead and do your work in advance so that you do not get behind. Then, just save the work and upload your postings during the appropriate week.

Icebreakers

Learners are not ready to work together on curricula unless inclusion and trust have been developed. Icebreakers are activities presented at the beginning of the course that help the learners present who they are, what they do well, and what their expectations, hopes, and needs might be. Not only are icebreakers used for getting to know each other but they also can be used as a lead-in for a topic or project. In the online classroom, icebreakers can be used to combine both. Taking the time to do icebreakers during the first week makes all the difference in building a community in which the students feel safe to learn and share personal thoughts.

It is important to remember that most online students are very busy people who are juggling work and family life and education. Icebreakers should be something they can do without a lot of personal thought or time. For example, you may ask students to post a very short bio of themselves and include one additional item to make it interesting, such as:

- Where they would travel in the world if they had unlimited funds and could pick just one location.
- Their favorite food, color, vacation spot, place to study, Internet site, and so on.
- How many children in their immediate family and if they are the first born, second, or baby.
- What their ultimate goal in education will be.
- What job they will have when they retire.
- Ways they like to relax.

If you have time in the course, it is always nice to be able to build in an icebreaker the first week of a course or group assignment to help the students get to know one another. Sometimes an icebreaker can also be added to an assignment. Here are some that the authors have used and enjoyed.

Joy

Objectives:
To give each learner the opportunity to share something special with others.
To practice "listening" skills.
To build community.

Instructions:

Ask each learner to think of three things that he or she

would like to share. Use the letters of the word "joy" to structure what to share.

J: something you *just* learned about another learner as you read the biographies.

O: *one* thing you hope to learn in this course.

Y: a quality *you* bring to this course.

After reading the posts, respond to each other's posts about commonalities.

Adapted from *Tribes* by Jeanne Gibbs, 1994

Meet Someone Special Objectives:

To introduce individuals to a community.

To build community inclusion.

To build self-esteem and appreciation for uniqueness.

Instructions:

This is a good activity to help learners introduce themselves to each other.

After reading the learner biographies, ask the learners to find someone they want to get to know better and form a partnership.

Have each partner interview the other.

At the end of the week, post an introduction to the group about your partner. Include the special things you learned through your interview.

Adapted from *Tribes* by Jeanne Gibbs, 1994

Dream Quilt

Objectives:

To build community inclusion.

To share a personal goal for the course.

Instructions:

This is an excellent strategy for starting off the course.

Have the learners read over the goals for the course and think of a personal goal they would like to achieve from participating in this course.

Write down the goal and why it was chosen. Post in the course room by Wednesday so other learners will have the opportunity to respond.

Respond to other learners about their goal.

Adapted from *Tribes* by Jeanne Gibbs, 1994

Group Icebreaker

Objectives:

To build community inclusion.

To share personal strengths.

Instructions:

Think about the skills that you bring to a team. Share and discuss these skills with your team in this thread. After discussing all of your skills, as a group come up with a team name that best describes you.

Communication Obstacles Icebreaker

Objectives:

To build community inclusion

To discuss obstacles to group work and how to overcome them.

Instructions:

Print and use the Challenge Card below, or create a card relevant to your particular group.

Working as a team, fill out the Challenge Card.

You may need to do it individually first and then compile all of the ideas to reach a consensus.

Team Name:

Names of Team Members:

List a common objective your team has in taking this course:

What are some of the obstacles you might face completing your group work?

List ways that these obstacles can be overcome:

Chapter Six

Nurturing the Novice Student

Danan Wylie was the instructor for the first class of my on-line master's degree program in 2006. I had no experience with on-line classes and I owe my success, in part, to her. She was always open, positive, and encouraging to all the students in our class. We were all new and struggling to learn the process of an on-line class, new to our master's degree program, and new to the requirements and demands of work, home, and school. Danan has a very special nurturing quality that helped us feel at ease. She always answered our questions promptly, she gave us examples, and she led us through our first class to successful completion. I must say, it is because of my positive experience in her class I believed I was prepared to go on. I am proud to say that I will complete my master's degree program and graduate in May 2008. I want to thank Danan for her part in giving me a great start in my on-line program. She would be a positive asset to any program or class.

- Jorga

Eventually, every instructor is asked to teach the first class in the degree program. This can be a big challenge. Students come in without knowing how to navigate the courseware. They are nervous and excited. This is a vital time of keeping the students in the class.

There are also times when you will have a class mixed with students who are seasoned as well as novice online learners. Sometimes the university will let you know this has happened, but other times this information may come out in the student biographies, if the student gets that far. Again, sending out a welcome email or e-card will reach these students and invite them in to the class. You may hear back from the novice students that they are nervous and new to online learning. Then you can offer the extra help they need to be successful.

The authors have had the pleasure of teaching these first time students in many different programs. We try to make sure that our students know that we care about them and their personal success. We are the "instructors with a heart". We want these new learners to know that we are here to support their success and transition to online learning and we are not here to "trick them up" or catch them in a mistake. We assure these new learners that if they make a mistake or overlook something important, we will give them the opportunity to make it right so they are well prepared for their next classes in the program.

Helping students navigate the course room

Preview weeks are great. Some universities provide the students with a preview week or a few days to explore the course room or course materials before the class actually begins. This time gives the student an opportunity to poke around in the classroom and learn to navigate through all of the links. This preview can be guided by the instructor to help the students learn the essential components of the classroom. If a preview is not provided by the university, this can still be done during the first week of class through a few structured activities led by the instructor. You might provide a scavenger hunt through the class or an optional or extra credit "quiz" over the syllabus and course expectations. A sample Scavenger Hunt exercise is shown below.

Scavenger Hunt

Participating in this scavenger hunt will help you learn how to navigate your classroom. It is important that you know where to look for various materials, how to ask questions, and how to send in materials for grading.

Over the first few days, find all of the following items. You will need to copy this page to a Word document and fill in the answers under each question. The final activity will be how to send the finished scavenger hunt to me. On Thursday of week 2, I will provide the answers.

1. *Where will you find the "Expectations for Week 1"? Name 3 things listed in "Expectations for Week 1".*
2. *Where can you find the information on the instructor? What are her online office hours?*
3. *Where can you find the break down of points? How did you get there?*
4. *Locate Module One. How many discussion questions are listed for the instructor to choose from?*
5. *Locate Lecture One. What are the main headings of this lecture?*
6. *Where will you find Online Library Access Instructions? What is the website address (URL) for the Grand Canyon library?*
7. *Where will you post an introduction of yourself?*
8. *How many peers do you need to respond to in a week? Can you just say you agree or disagree?*
9. *Where can you get messages from classmates and the instructor within the classroom? How do you get there?*
10. *Where can you find your grades? How do you get there?*
11. *Where is the assignments box? How do you get there?*
12. *What is listed in the "nuts and bolts" discussion strand? Name 2 items you will use.*
13. *After answering all of the above questions, save this document to a folder that you create for this class on your hard drive. Go to the assignment's box. Find the scavenger hunt assignment. Click on it. Attach your document and send. You have successfully submitted an assignment! Please keep these directions for your use in sending future documents.*

Send a welcome note

As stated in previous chapters, sending welcome notes and words of encouragement to the students is very important. These novice students need your feedback more than experienced online students do. The first week of class, posting a general note to everyone is a nice touch.

I just wanted to tell you how thrilled I am with the quality of your discussion posts. The responses to each other are also very well done. I like how you are adding personal experiences and knowledge to the discussions. Some of you are even adding information from books and journals. This is great! Keep up the good work!

Absent students

About mid-week, you may have some students who have not yet made an appearance. A personal email will usually tell you whether or not they have changed their mind or just need a little prodding.

Hi,

I noticed that you have not yet joined the class in our discussions and wanted to know what I can do to help you get started. I remember how intimidating it is to begin learning in a new environment. I am here to help you. If you need help logging in to the classroom, tech support may be able to help you. If you have other concerns, please let me know how I can help. You can call me at (123)456-7890 or email me at dmyerswylie@cox.net. I look forward to hearing from you soon.

Hi,

I am looking forward to your participation in the discussion room soon. If there is something, you do not understand or you are, feeling overwhelmed please feel free to contact me and we can discuss any concerns you have. I remember my first week in the online classroom and I had so many questions. I understand the fears and concerns that students may have. I am here to help you. My email is dhardy@yah11.com *and my telephone is (123)456-7890. I am looking forward to hearing from you!*

Tips and Tricks Section

Through trial and error, we have learned that we need to provide the students with the tools to be successful. We provide a section in the classroom that has "tips and tricks." Some examples of information to include in this section are given below: however, not all of these are applicable or appropriate for every class or program. It is important that you are familiar with the University handbook and catalog to ensure the information you provide does not contradict this information.

1. A sample paper that is formatted correctly using the format the university requires.
   a. **APA**: psychology, education, and other social sciences.
   b. **MLA**: literature, arts, and humanities.
   c. **AMA**: medicine, health, and biological sciences.
   d. **Turabian**: designed for college students to use with all subjects.
   e. **Chicago**: used with all subjects in the "real world" by books, magazines, newspapers, and other non-scholarly publications.
2. A definition of plagiarism and cheating.
3. Writing format tips sheet.
4. How to write citations and references.
5. Help for APA references and citations
6. How to respond to discussion questions.
7. What is a substantive discussion question response?
8. Information on the portfolio requirements.
9. Why not to use online encyclopedias such as Wikipedia.

10. Netiquette guidelines
11. What I look for when I grade your work.
12. Copies of the rubrics used for grading.
13. Templates for assignments.
14. Samples of assignments.
15. How to search on the Internet.
16. How to use the library.

Below are samples of some of the items the authors put in their tips and tricks section:

Internet search engines

I am convinced that Google Scholar is absolutely the finest search engine for scholarly literature available on the web. There are dozens of other sources for scholarly literature, of course (some that require paid subscriptions like XanEdu), but for ease of search terms and sheer numbers of articles available in just seconds, I recommend using Google Scholar first so that you save yourself search time. It sure beats going through dusty stacks of books at a university library and getting dirty fingers while having one's asthma flare up (Griffis, 2007)!

Information from Google Scholar itself, "Google Scholar enables you to search specifically for scholarly literature, including peer-reviewed papers, theses, books, preprints, abstracts and technical reports from all broad areas of research. Use Google Scholar to find articles from a wide variety of academic publishers, professional societies, preprint repositories, and universities, as well as scholarly articles available across the web."

Google Scholar is Free

Anyone can access the Google Scholar search engine directly through Google or by clicking on the link below:

http://scholar.google.com/

Techniques to help you search are called Boolean techniques.

To search for two or more terms on the same page, type the word AND between the terms.

To search for two or more terms on the same page, type the word OR between the terms.

To search for pages that include the first term and not the second, type the words AND NOT between the terms.

To search for an exact phrase, enclose the phrase in quotation marks.

To group parts of your search, enclose that part in parentheses.

To search for various forms of a word, add an asterisk to the end of the word.

If you want the search engine to search for all of the words you enter, put the '+'symbol between the words.

School Library

There is a link to the online library on your course page. You can search for a variety of items. Most of the time you will be searching for journals.

After accessing your online library, select, "find articles" on one of your databases. The usual database used to search for articles is Academic Search Premier.

To search for a specific journal, type the name of the journal in the "FIND" box. Under the "FIND" box will be a "Default Fields" box. Then look below the search boxes to the

"Limit Your Results" area and click on the box for "Full Text." Click the "Search" button. The specific journal, if in the database, will come up.

You can begin a search by typing in a topic. Use the Boolean techniques to help with the search. Sometimes, a search may result in bringing up too many articles. This is when you will need to narrow your search by using specific words. For example, you may begin a search for online instruction. This brings up over 1,000 articles. Ask yourself what specifically you would like to know about online instruction. Type the specific topic in the "FIND" box under "Limit your results" to narrow your search.

To narrow this search to a journal, under "Limit your results," add a specific article name or author by putting the author's name in the "FIND" box. This will narrow the search to articles written by the author in that journal. You can do the same with the title. This search will find articles with the subject in the specified journal.

If you begin a search, and too few results are found, or no results, think about how you can widen your search. For example, when searching for Critical Thinking in Online Instruction, you may come up with only one article. Broaden this search by asking for teaching strategies in online instruction.

Netiquette

Netiquette is etiquette of cyberspace. It is a set of rules for proper online behavior. Often times, people get on the Internet and forget that there is a human being receiving the message being sent. The message may be offensive or taken in a different manner than it was intended. Most people would rather make friends than enemies. When communicating in the online classroom, your words are written. The words are there for everyone to see; which could come back to haunt you. Before posting, ask yourself, "Would I say this to the person's face?" If the answer is no, then rewrite and reread the message until the message is something that you could say to the person face to face. If you follow a few basic rules, you are less likely to make mistakes.

The most important rule to remember is the golden rule: Do unto others, as you would want them to do unto you.

* *Avoid using all caps. IT LOOKS LIKE YOU ARE SHOUTING*
* *Avoid posting unrelated comments or advertisements. This is called Spamming.*
* *Avoid passing around chain letters or e-Hoaxes.*

* *Avoid sending hate-filled messages, being rude, or expressing outrage.*

* *Avoid the use of irony and sarcasm. It may come across as confusing or rude.*

Definition of Plagiarism

Many students do not know the definition of plagiarism (aka academic dishonesty). In my experience, most plagiarism is not intentional. It is important, especially when we do the majority of our research online, to learn about academic dishonesty as well as ways to avoid it. Plagiarism is the use of material that is not your own. Students are expected to be honest and ethical in their academic work by properly citing any sources used.

With cutting and pasting of information from Internet sites, it is too easy to put together a paper using various websites and present it as your own work without referencing the sources. There are a several websites that sell graduate and undergraduate papers. There are also just as many websites to find out if there is plagiarism in your papers. Turning in a plagiarized paper can result in the end of your academic career. Even paraphrasing other sources can be picked up by search engines as well as websites utilized to find plagiarism. Even if you copy and paste a section of a website and then revise it to make it appear to be your own work, you must give the source that the information came from.

Ways to avoid Academic Dishonesty

Students who choose to learn online often do so because it fits into their already hectic lives. These students do not have the time to travel across town, find parking, and attend scheduled classes. Coupled with already busy lives, learners add the pressures of academia, which may cause many online learners to become overwhelmed or pressured to complete assignments. This is when dishonesty can occur. The following strategies can help learners avoid unintentional academic dishonesty.

· Do not procrastinate.

· Set aside enough time to do your best on assignments and study for tests.

· Include time to complete other activities for your family, yourself, and work.

· Find a tutor or form a study group to help in areas that are particularly difficult.

· Summarize sources you will use by making annotated bibliographies.

· If you use another person's words or ideas, you must give that person credit as the source

Information on APA

Scholarly Paper Guidelines & Checklist
Written by Dr. Alisa Griffis
Font and Size: Use Times New Roman, 12 point (Courier is okay, but not a great choice)

Cover Page: Put a cover page on everything you turn in.
Page Breaks: Put a hard page break between major sections of your papers, including the cover sheet and the text, as well as the text and any references. This is created by a very simple command in Microsoft Word: Control + Enter (just place your cursor where the page break should go and do (Control + Enter) and you will get a hard page break.

Headers: Put a header with a short title (not your name) and page numbers in the upper right-hand corner of EVERY scholarly paper. In Word, you do this by clicking "view" on your toolbar and then "header and footer".
Double-Spacing: Double space the body of your paper -- the only thing that will be single-spaced is the references...with a double-space in between. To change papers from single-spaced to double spaced in Microsoft Word, go to your toolbar and click "Format" then "Paragraph" then change "single" to "double" spacing, then click "Okay."

Justification: Left-justified, right margin not justified.

Margins: 1" all the way around. APA style says that you must have even margins (not 1.25" on the left).

Headings: Your first main heading (like "Introduction") would be centered with the first letters of main words being capitalized (no bold or underline):

Introduction

Secondary headings (those that fall in between main, centered headings) are flush left, italicized, with Upper Case and Lower Case words like this:

Examining Musical Instruments

In rare cases, you may have a third level of headings (not likely). If you were to have one or two in a paper (for example, some heading that falls under the "Examining Musical Instruments" topic and the next main topic, all falling within the "Introduction" category, it would be written as an indented, italicized, heading with lower case words (only the first word would be capitalized) and would end in a period.

Timeframe for the examination of the instruments.

Regular Indentation: Indent your paragraphs using the "Tab" key (do NOT space in five spaces). Do NOT "block" indent your normal text and do not put an extra space in between paragraphs. Just simple, normal double-spaced text and indented paragraphs.

Block Indentation: Any direct quote of 40 words or over must be block indented, double spaced, with no quotation marks. Indent these block-indented quotes ½" from the left margin.

Bold, Underline, Color: Never use bold or underline or color in your APA papers - even if the sample shows bold or underline! You will use italics within your reference pages to show book titles or journal names, but within your text - never. APA is very boring that way!

Bullets: No bullets of any sort are allowed in formal APA papers (you are allowed to number stuff lists, however!).

Numbered Lists: Keep any numbered lists short – if you have more than one sentence in each individually numbered list, you would be better off paraphrasing and discussing it within the text. If you are quoting a previously bulleted section from a scholarly paper or book and there are more than 40 words, be sure to block indent it.

General Rules for Good Paper Writing

Use varied sentence structure. Do not repeat words or phrases within paragraphs if possible. Begin each sentence within each paragraph with a different word. Do not overuse words throughout your paper. Check for this after you believe you are finished with your final draft.

Grammar, Usage, Mechanics, and Punctuation: As a matter of professional integrity, all credentialed, certificated, and/or licensed instructors getting a master's degree in education should carefully proofread each scholarly paper for accuracy in word choice and correct spelling and punctuation. Do not rely solely upon spell check and grammar check. It often cannot identify incorrectly chosen words (such as "loose" or "lose" or "choice" or "choose").

Paraphrasing: Paraphrase at least ¾ of the information that you find from other sources. Do not just "switch around the words" – this is considered plagiarism. Instead, discuss the essence of the materials and put it into your own words.

References and In-Text Citations

In-Text Citations: Correct examples of in-text citations:

Example One (paraphrased):

Griffis (2006) indicated there were several APA points to remember when writing and editing a paper.

Example Two (paraphrased):

There are several APA points to remember when writing and editing a paper (Griffis, 2006).
Example Three (direct quote):

"When writing in the APA style, one must not use bold or underline in the topic headings or the body of the text, and there must be a header on each paper" (Griffis, 2006, p. 7).

Note that the first two examples are paraphrased and a page number is therefore unnecessary.

Note that the third example is a direct quote and therefore must have a page number in the in-text citation.

Also: Examine Example #3 carefully. Note that the period goes *outside* the parentheses, *not* at the end of the sentence.

In-Text Citation Rule-of-Thumb #1: Approximately two-thirds to three-fourths of your in-text citations should be written in the general style of examples #1 and #2. Only about one-fourth of your in-text citations should be direct quotes. Why? Because when we paraphrase, we are displaying higher order thinking skills and sound scholarly thought processes. Over use of direct quotes is somewhat of a cop-out and displays lesser scholarly aptitude.

In-Text Citation Rule-of-Thumb #2: When picking between Example #1 and Example #2 for in-text citations, lean more heavily upon Example #2.

References: The Publication Manual of the American Psychological Association (5th Edition) lists virtually every possible combination of references possible. Refer to this book for details. In general, however, references should look like this:

Book Reference:

Paivio, A., & Harris, W. (2006). *Imagery and verbal processing.* New York: Hold, Reinhart & Winston.

Journal Reference from a paper journal: Eysenck, M.W. (2003). Extraversion, verbal learning, and memory. *American Journal of Psychology, 83*(7) 75-90.

Journal Reference from an Online Source (and this is identical to the one that was published in the paper journal):

Eysenck, M.W. (2003). Extraversion, verbal learning, and memory. [Electronic version]. *American Journal of Psychology, 83*(7) 75-90.

Journal Reference from an Online Source such as an electronic-only journal OR an article that may have been modified or altered from the original that was published previously: Eysenck, M.W. (2003). Extraversion, verbal learning, and memory. *American Journal of Psychology, 83*(7) 75-90. Retrieved October 31, 2007, from http://www.americanjofpsych.com

Hanging Indent for References: ALL references should have a hanging indent. This is easy to create. Type in your references, then highlight them all, and move the bottom triangle of your horizontal tool bar over to the .5" mark.

To see an example of the toolbar ruler's correct configuration, you may drag your cursor over and then click on any of the four reference examples above and then watch the toolbar above move to the "hanging indent" position.

Scholarly Paper Checklist

_____ Font and Size: I have used Times New Roman, 12 point, throughout my paper.

_____ Cover Page: My cover page is double-spaced & centered.

_____ Page Breaks: I have hard page breaks between my cover sheet & text and between my text & reference page.

_____ Headers: I have a header in the upper left-hand page. It does not list my name but instead lists the key words of my title. The page numbers are there as well.

_____ Double-Spacing: My paper is double-spaced throughout.

_____ Justification: My paper is left justified.

_____ Margins: I have 1" margins all the way around.

_____ Headings: I have appropriately centered main headings and any secondary or tertiary headings are appropriately configured.

_____ Regular Indentation: I indented ½ inch from the margin using the "tab" key.

_____ Block Indentation: I block indented ½ inch for direct quotes of 40 words or more.

_____ Bold, Underline, Color: I do not have these in my paper.

_____ Bullets: There are not bullets in my paper.

_____ Numbered Lists: I have kept my numbered lists short, if there are any.

_____ Varied Sentence Structure: I have checked each paragraph for varied sentence structure.

_____ Grammar, Usage, Mechanics, and Punctuation: I have run spell check and grammar check AND I have read each sentence independently checking for misused words or awkward sentences.

_____ Paraphrasing: I have appropriately paraphrased about 75% of my in-text citations.

_____ In-Text Citations: I have checked my in-text citations for correct APA style and punctuation.

_____ References: My references have a hanging indent. They are punctuated properly. They are capitalized properly according to the examples here and also in the APA Publication Manual.

Expectations for participation

To clearly and completely answer a question, a post should be anywhere between one hundred and three hundred words. A rule of thumb for the length of an initial post to a discussion question should be that the reader does not have to toggle down the page more than once to read the entire post.

Make sure that posts are not too long. Stick to the topic. Think about what you want to say, get the ideas straight, do the research and document with facts, and read and reread your posts to ensure that the post is clear and concise before posting.

The likelihood of a peer reading an extremely long post in its entirety is low. A post that is longer than one hundred words should be broken into paragraphs. Skip a line between paragraphs for readability.

Make all posts within the courseware. In other words, do not use attachments. Most attachments go unread. The only attachments that should be used are to post rough drafts and final copies of group and individual projects.

How to respond to discussion questions

I know a lot of you are new to online learning. I remember my first class was very stressful. I want to make this as easy for you as possible.

It is very easy for discussion questions to get buried in the discussion board. For week 1, there is only 1 question. In future weeks, you may have 2 discussion questions, so pay close attention to how this is done:

I want to make sure that all of you get credit for your posting. Please do not use the "add new thread" button at the top of the page. When making your initial response to the discussion questions, use the following steps:

1. *Locate the discussion question in the week one discussions thread and open the question up.*
2. *Click on the "reply" button found on the right of the screen.*
3. *Change the subject to read: "your name, DQ # __ "*
4. *Write your answer to the question and hit submit.*

To respond to another learner, use the following steps:

1. *Open up the learner's original post and click "reply".*
2. *In the subject line, type: "to _____ ".*
3. *Type your response and submit.*

Remember, you need to answer all discussion questions (only 1 during week 1 and a minimum of 2 responses to your peers each week. During week 1, you should also spend time reading and responding to each other's introductions and try out the icebreaker. Responding to each other's introductions and the icebreaker will help you to get to know each other and give you an idea of whom you would like to work with when we break into groups for our group projects.

What I look for when grading your papers

Some tips on how to get the best grade on your papers. These are the things I look for in grading your papers.

One is that you have covered all the points of the assignment. Each assignment has a list of items that need to be addressed. They are listed in the assignment area. I also look for the quality of the response.

The next thing is to check to see if you are using the proper APA format in your paper, the length of the paper, and how easy it is to follow.

The last item is I will periodically check your references with your document and run them through Safe Assignments. Safe Assignments is a tool that you can use to see if papers have any places that need to be cited. It will show the sources that were copied. I strongly suggest that you read the information on APA and how to properly cite and reference sources.

Chapter Seven

Creating Good Course Discussion

Donna was great--she was very helpful and continued to provide encouragement throughout the course!

Many universities have curriculum writers who write the courses. You receive the materials already set up in the course room. Some give you a list of discussion questions to choose from while others provide the questions you must ask the students. Either way a good instructor can feel limited in their ability to reach higher levels of interaction and learning. In this chapter, we will discuss tips to have good, quality discussions that delve beyond a cursory response to the discussion questions.

Be active

It is important to be active in the discussions. Just reading the student posts does not let the students see your presence. This puts you behind the scenes instead of center stage. When this happens, students write only what they already know; not expanding on their learning. A good rule of thumb is to respond to at least 1 person per day, 4 to 5 days a week. Remember, you are the content expert and must help to guide the discussions to enable the students to expand their knowledge on the subject.

Be a good role model

The instructor must model what is expected in an initial response as well as in responses to peers within a given discussion. To do this, the instructor can answer the first question of the first week of the course. The instructor can answer the first question of the first week of the course. Give a good, solid response to the question. Go beyond just answering the question by bringing in some research on the subject. This can be directly from the reading. Finally, show application of the information to your own life and/or profession. This gives the students a solid example of what is expected in the discussions. Here is an example from a Business course on organizational management.

Question:
How do organizations communicate?

Answer:
Many organizations have unique communication systems in place. Most organizations have formal and informal channels.
Formal channels are those planned and set up by the organization. One example is downward communication. This is when a message is sent from the manager to the followers. If the employees communicate with the manager this would be an upward communication. The manager and peers or coworkers would use horizontal communication.
The informal channels can include the grapevine and it travels fast. Networking is another way of information communication.

Create active participation through participation

Active participation by the instructor is necessary to stimulate deeper and more meaningful discussions. Again, when the instructor responds to the students, s/he is giving the student an example of what is expected in a response. Within the first two days of a course, a good instructor should respond to at least one student. This response should have many of the same components of an initial response with one change; it adds to the discussion thread that has been started by the students. It can begin several different ways:

1.   In this example from a discussion board on nursing, the instructor begins with quoting the part of the student's response that will be addressed:

"In nursing, it is important to make sure that we protect ourselves from communicable diseases."

2.   Begin with agreeing with something that is said in the student's response.

I agree that nurses need to protect themselves form communicable diseases.

3.   Begin with stating what the student said and asking a question for further information.

In what ways can we protect ourselves?

After the beginning, there are several things that you can do to stimulate more discussion.

1.   In this example from an engineering class, the instructor brings in research and then how it applies to the profession.

Research shows that there is a high stress factor for engineers because of the many conflicting demands and expectations of the job (Myers, 2005).

2.   Give examples. Here is one from a writing class.

I totally agree that when writing a report, a good writer begins with an outline. The writer will use the outline to begin writing a rough draft. This draft will go through several stages of editing and proofreading before it becomes a final project.

Give the students choices

Another way to create active participation is to give the students several choices of questions to answer. When a list of discussion questions are given for the instructor to choose from, make one question the main discussion. Then list all of the rest and give the students a choice of which question they would like to answer.

In using this strategy, the students' interests are held because there is a wider amount of information covered. Here is an example from an education course:

Discussion Questions

Please respond to the first question and then choose one of the other questions to respond. After your first two initial responses, please revisit the discussion board to respond to a minimum of two of your peers.

1. *What strategies do you think are most effective in teaching reading comprehension?*
2. *Choose one of the following questions to answer:*
   a. *What is reading comprehension? What problems do your students face in reading comprehension?*
   b. *What are your views on phonics vs. whole language instruction for teaching reading? Why?*
   c. *Why is written expression the most difficult of all academic skills to master?*
   d. *In what ways can technology be used to teach students reading and written language? Share relevant programs or websites.*

Add a question

As an active part of the discussion, an instructor knows when a good discussion begins to become redundant. This is the time to bring in more questions. Go back to the provided list of questions and pull out another question to post on the board. Here is an example from a computer course:

The class has been discussing the different types of web browsers. Midweek the instructor notices that everyone has responded with similar responses. This does not allow for discussion and needs to be revitalized by adding a question.
Please answer the following question:

I noticed that the majority of you favor Firefox over Internet Explorer. Give a personal example of why this browser is superior.

A third question can be added to continue the conversation:

Go to the Firefox website. Read about this browser. Then write down how you would explain how Firefox is superior to a person that does not understand web browsers.

Know your material

Another way to stimulate a stagnate discussion forum, is to review the weekly material and find a nugget to post for student response. Many textbook publishers are online. Often you can see if the book has additional information available. You can often find PowerPoint presentations that add excellent points to the discussions or you may find a recap of the week's reading to add into the discussion. Often these may be a different view on the subject. This will bring the students back into the discussions and heighten your participation.

One other effective way to stimulate discussion is to do a search of the web for supplemental material. Due to copy write laws, give the link to the students for review. It is not mandatory reading, but is given as help for them in creating their professional toolbox or portfolio. If you plan to teach the same class often, you will want to create a list of this supplemental material for ease of access in the future.

Learners are always looking for new ideas, techniques, and strategies. By adding a second or even a third question to the discussion board, the students will begin to check back to read what their peers are writing. Something will spur them and they will begin to participate in the discussion.

There are times that you will need to write your own or edit the given discussion questions. In so doing, you want to make sure that you are reaching higher levels of critical thinking. You want to get your students to analyze, synthesize, and evaluate material rather than simply recalling and comprehending.

Analysis (taking apart the known)

- Can you compare your….with that presented in ….?
- Can you explain what must have happened when….?
- Can you distinguish between …..?
- How is ….similar to….?
- What was the underlying theme of….?
- What do you see as other possible outcomes?
- What are some of the problems of….?
- What was the turning point in the game?
- What was the problem with…?
- Which events could have happened….?
- Synthesis (putting things together in another way)
- Can you design a…..to….?
- Can you see a possible solution to….?
- Can you create new and unusual uses for….?
- Can you write a new recipe for a tasty dish?
- Can you develop a proposal that would….?
- How many ways can you….?
- If you had access to all resources how would you deal with….?
- What would happen if….?
- Why not compose a song about….?
- Why don't you devise your own way to deal with….?
- Evaluation (judging outcomes)
- Can you defend your position about….?
- Do you think….is a good or a bad thing? Explain your answer.
- How would you have handled….?
- How would you feel if….?
- How effective are….?
- Judge the value of….
- What changes to….would you recommend? Explain your answer.

Chapter Eight

Collaboration

Collaboration is an essential part of the online learning environment that separates this type of learning from independent learning or self-paced learning. The goal of having students work together in partners or small groups is to help them develop and exchange ideas with each other. By doing so, the students see other points of view which enables them to learn more by seeing the subject through another person's eyes.

Forming small groups is one way to deliberately promote collaboration. Students may feel more inclined to share personal experiences or try new strategies in a small group situation rather than a whole class discussion. Small groups help to engage the learners in an interactive approach to processing information which can improve retention of course material, improve motivation, and help group members get to know one another. Groups can be formed for several reasons: to engage in small-group discussions, to complete group assignments, and do group activities.

Group Activities

Group activities require collaboration by all members of a group. Small groups can collaborate on assignments, create projects, conduct brainstorming sessions, discuss course readings, create projects, work on case studies, critique each other's work, or just about any activity that requires the exchanging of ideas among peers.

The members should be active in the development and decision-making process of the group activity. A good group activity should:

1. Allow time for team-building
2. Encourage positive group skills
3. Be more than questions and answers
4. Be content-focused
5. Require learners to respond to each other
6. Build on each others' thoughts
7. Require group members to use critical thinking
8. Have clear and explicit directions
9. Produce an end product (Conrad and Donaldson, 2004)

Types of group activities

Case study

Case studies are great ways to apply learning. In a case study, students are given or asked to construct a real-life problem relevant to the course. Well-chosen problems encourage students to define problems, identify what information is needed, engage in solution, and decision-making. Students work through the case with their group and present the case to the class. This can lead to a discussion of the case, which helps the remainder of the class learn from the group experience.

Debates

In an online environment, formal debates can take place by dividing the class into teams and assigning each team a specific argument or position. Prior to assigning the debate, the learners need to know the expectations and guidelines for good debating. These guidelines include:

1. Questions or challenges should be professional. Critical analysis, synthesis, rhetorical skill, and wit are keys to debate success.
2. Focus on the opposing side's position or argument.
3. Limit your arguments to three or less.

4. *Use logic to make your arguments. Present these arguments clearly and concisely.*

5. *Present the content accurately. Only use content that is pertinent to your point of view and draw on support from authoritative sources.*

6. *Be certain of the validity of all external evidence presented for your arguments. In addition, challenges to the validity of evidence should be made only on substantive grounds.*

7. *Your rebuttal (or conclusion) in a debate is your final summary position. Use it as an opportunity to highlight important issues that indicate proof of your points or refute your opponent's argument. (Friedman, Joseph, Schubart, Sheridan, and Wyatt, 2002)*

Facilitating the discussion

Facilitating the discussion provides learners with a sense of empowerment that "is both a critical element and a desired outcome of participation in an online learning community" (Palloff & Pratt, 1999). Having learners facilitate shifts the knowledge from the instructor to the learners. The group becomes the "expert" on the topic. By rotating the facilitation students become responsible for community building

Presentations

Presentation software is used for presenting information in a dynamic slide show format. Text, charts, graphs, sound, and video are just some of the features that presentation software can incorporate into a presentation. Learners can be given the option to present their group project using presentation software. Adding the use of a microphone or a video recorder, a group can also add audio and video to the presentation.

Vignettes

A vignette is a short, descriptive literary review or scene de-

signed by the instructor. (Wines & Bianchi, n.d.) The group is invited to leave behind the reality of the present and enjoy the freedom of imagining the possibilities of this scenario. Through a presentation, project, or paper the group shares their dreams and ideas with the class. Through collaboration, the class can then begin to turn these dreams of what could be possible into solutions and strategies that can begin to be adopted today.

1. Summaries
2. Reviews
3. Team Performance Logs

The team performance log is a way to keep track of group work in progress. In each group, a group leader is assigned. All members of the group fill out weekly summaries and send it to the leader to compile and send to the instructor. Some of the items a team performance log may have are:

1. what you have been doing
2. how much time it took you
3. what you have found out
4. what difficulties you have encountered (Newman, 2003)

Graphic organizers/mind maps

Graphic organizers and mind maps can be used as a visual representation of the learning from a group. For example, a group may want to research and discuss a topic within their small group. The graphic organizer or mind map may be their way of demonstrating the information to the class.

Role-plays

Learners bring their own experiences to the online learning community. Online role-play explicitly takes advantage of these life experiences by having learners step into the shoes of others. When learners play a role different from their everyday roles, the *learners receive new insights about that role. The online course room allows time for the learners to research and reflect on the roles. The learners can also rehearse as a group what they will present to the class. (Ip, 2004)*

Dividing Students into Groups

Groups can be formed by the instructor or the students. The writers caution you on allowing students to form their own groups as it can be quite time consuming, something we do not have in the fast-pace online course, and inevitably, there is not an equitable split among group size without input from the faculty member. The only time this approach works very well is in a course where all of the students know each other. It is a best practice to allow students to make group requests before assigning teams. The authors often invite the students to make team requests a few days before the teams are to be assigned, but do so with the disclaimer that while requests will be accommodated if possible, there are no guarantees. Faculty members should ensure that the students privately email their requests in order to not hurt anyone's feelings for not being included in a group.

A good way to form groups is to use the biographies that students post the first day or two of class. Here is a prompt for the biographies used in a Master's of Education course:

In the first day or two of class, please tell us a little about yourself, both professionally and personally. Please include where you live and work, what grade level you teach, how long you have been teaching, and why you have chosen to go back to school at this time. Let us get to know the "real you" behind the words on the screen.

This biography gives the instructor the necessary information to form groups several different ways. Groups can be formed by time zones, grade level and/or content expertise, and personal commonalities. The most common and easiest way to form groups is by time zones.

PST	MT	CST	EST	Other
Jim	Nicole	Andrea	Michael	Sarah (Korea)
Debbie	Jennifer	David	Kimberly	Joan (Jamaica)
Keith		Robert	Schona	
		Diane	Karen	
		Samantha	Kathy	
			Cindy	

With the above chart of time zones, four groups could be formed with four to five in each group. The goal is to keep the students closest to the same time zones as possible and keep the groups to no less than three and no more than five students. The groups for this class would look something like this:

Group 1	Group 2	Group 3	Group 4
Sarah	Nicole	Robert	Michael
Jim	Jennifer	Diane	Kimberly
Debbie	Andrea	Samantha	Schona
Keith	David	Kathy	Karen
		Cindy	Joan

Another way to form groups is by the students' professional experience. In the master's of education example above, students could be paired by grade level taught. This way is more complicated and you will find that students are all in different time zones, which make it more difficult for students to be online at the same time. However, for some assignments, this type of grouping may be more appropriate for some assignments and it can be done.

Kinder-garten	3-Jan	6-Apr	9-Jul	12-Oct	Non-instruc-tors
Debbie	Jennifer	Andrea	Jim	Keith	Nicole
Michael	Kathy	David	Robert	Diana	Karen
		Saman-tha	Joan	Kimberly	
		Schona		Cindy	
				Sarah	

With the grade level division, an instructor runs into the difficulty of where to place the non-teaching students unless you have an insight into what grade level they hope to teach after receiving their degree. Here is how the groups would form by grade levels.

K-3	4-6	7-10	10-12
Debbie	Andrea	Jim	Diana
Michael	David	Robert	Kimberly
Jennifer	Samantha	Joan	Sarah
Kathy	Schona	Cindy	Nicole
Karen		Keith	

The final way and far more difficult way to form groups would be by personal commonalities. However, this may be necessary in certain types of courses. For example, when teaching a course where students are changing careers or preparing for a career, they may not have specific categories to divide into like the grade levels above. You may want to divide them by their interested career path. Take a business administration course for example:

Human Resources	Technical	Banking and Commerce	Administration
Debbie	Jim	Michael	Karen
Diana	Robert	David	Schona
Kathy	Cindy	Keith	Jennifer
Samantha	Joan	Kimberly	Nicole
Andrea	Sarah		

One frustrating problem will be the students who do not enter the classroom within the first few days or do not respond to the biography prompt. Through successes and failures, the best way to handle this situation is to pad the groups with the no-shows. It is easier to take a student out of a group than it is to put them in one once the groups have been formed and are working. Of course, you have no information on the student so it would be the best guess of the instructor as to which group to put them in. By no means should another group be formed with all of the no shows. This will backfire with only one or two late students checking in, making group work difficult and much more time consuming for them and you.

Getting Groups Started

In most eight-week courses, collaborative projects begin the second or third week. Do not wait until the beginning of that week to put your students into groups. The earlier you can get the students divided into groups, the better. This allows the students adequate time to get to know their teammates, share alternate contact information, and discuss and agree upon team policies and procedures for successful group work. Post the groups and the first assignment as soon as possible, even if it is before the beginning of that week's assignment. Let's look at the following scenarios:

Scenario 1

The first collaborative assignment is given during week two. Groups are formed by day five of week one. A note is sent out to the class:

Hi Everyone,

Thank you all for responding to the biography! I have enjoyed reading about each of you. I hope that you all take time to read through the bios to get to know your fellow students.

The information you provided helped to form your collaborative learning group. Your first assignment is in week 2. If you go to your course content page, you will find a folder with your name on it. Click on that folder. Inside you will find the first assignment posted as well as a forum for discussion and sharing of your projects. I urge all of you to visit your group area as soon as possible to introduce yourself to your team members and get started.

Working in groups can be very challenging in the online forum. For that reason, I have taken into consideration the extra time it will take to complete this assignment. You have access to your project now, two days before the week begins. You will also have three extra days to complete the assignment. This first group assignment will be due on Wednesday of week 3. Please try to adhere to the following timeline in completing your group project:

Monday:	*Introductions made*
Wednesday:	*Division of the assignment*
Saturday:	*Post your portion of the assignment*
Monday:	*Rough draft of completed group assignment posted to discussion board for editing and comments from group*
Tuesday:	*Final copy posted to discussion board for group approval*
Wednesday:	*Assignment due in assignments folder*

If you have any questions, please do not hesitate to ask. Please use the "questions for instructor" forum as someone else may have the same question as you.

Scenario 2

Assignment is to be completed in week seven. This assignment is worth 20% of the grade and is a huge assignment. For this class, groups are formed by the end of week two. The following note is sent out to the class at the beginning of week three:

Hi Everyone,

Thank you all for responding to the biography! I have enjoyed reading about each of you. I hope that you all take time to read through the bios to get to know your fellow students.

The information you provided helped to form your collaborative learning group. Your first assignment is in week 2. If you go to your course content page, you will find a folder with your name on it. Click on that folder. Inside you will find the first assignment posted as well as a forum for discussion and sharing of your projects. I urge all of you to visit your group area as soon as possible to introduce yourself to your team members and get started.

Working in groups can be very challenging in the online forum. For that reason, I have taken into consideration the extra time it will take to complete this assignment. You have access to your project now and will begin the project during week 3, even though it is not in the course materials until week 7. I am doing this for a reason. First, this project is worth 20% of your grade. In addition, a huge project takes a lot of pre-organization by the group. We will begin this organization now to give the group members time to work on their project throughout the class. This assignment will be posted in the class discussion forum on Tuesday of week 8.

For this week, you need to begin making some group decisions.

1. *Select a group leader that will be the person that communicates with me.*
2. *In your groups, decide the grade level you wish to use for your thematic unit. It can be a range of grades such as Pre-k – kinder, first-third, fourth- sixth, seventh-ninth, and tenth-twelfth. Or it can be an individual grade level.*
3. *Select the topic of your unit. Some that I have received in the past are marine life, The Civil War, Colors, and Plants. You need to choose a unit that you can make a variety of lesson plans including Language Arts, Music, Art, PE, and Social Studies or Science.*
4. *You will all use the SIOP model for this unit. I will provide you with a template and sample lesson plan.*

The group leader will email the grade level and topic to the instructor by the end of the week. If you have any questions, please do not hesitate to ask. Please use the "questions for instructor" forum as someone else may have the same question as you.

Scenario 3

The first group project is due at the end of workshop three. Groups are formed at the beginning of week two. The following message is sent to the students:

Hi Everyone,

You have all been divided into groups for your group projects. Your first group project will be completed during week three. I always like to give groups plenty of time to get organized for their assignments. So your assignment is posted. During week two, take a few minutes to get into your groups, introduce yourself to your group, read the assignment, and begin to divide the assignment between all of you. Please do not hesitate to jump in and take charge.

Group Problems

Some students do not like group work in the online class-room. The students have difficulty trusting that the assignment will be completed in the time allotted. That is one good reason to give extra time for group projects by either posting the assignments early or moving the due date back several days.

Nevertheless, even with some proactive planning and accommodation on the part of the instructor, group work issues can and do arise. So, how do you handle problems that arise within groups and between members? When do you get involved? Let's look at some scenarios:

Scenario 1:

In this scenario, the student fails to actively participate in the group project to which he is assigned and other members of group complain to you, asking that he be removed from the group.

For this scenario, the authors would do two separate posts: one in a private email to the student, and a second one in the group discussion area for the entire group to see. Why would we want to place a second one in the group area instead of just sending one to the student? This second posting shows the group that you are addressing the issue. The private email can be more direct to that one student.

Hi _____,

I just took a peek in your group discussions and noticed that you have not yet made an appearance. Can I help? The group project has already begun and is due at the end of this week. I hope that you will find time soon to pop into your group and take part in this activity. The rubric for group projects is posted in the course room. Half of the points for the group project are participation. This project is worth 10 points. Losing 5 points will lower your grade possibly one whole grade. Please let me know what I can do to help. Remember, I am here to help you be successful.

Dear Group,

As l member of a small group .please realize that your participation is essential to the group. Although we can all learn independently, we learn exponentially when working collaboratively. We all come from different backgrounds in life with many different skills and expertise to share with the group. Each of you brings more diversity into the classroom to help by building a community of learners. You are working for a common purpose. However, in order to for this to be successful, we need to have participation by all members of the group. Participation by all students is expected.

Scenario 2:

In this scenario, a student is disgruntled with the final project that was submitted by the group and sends out an email to all group members. The one group member that took the time to put the group project together responded back to the whole group stating that she even waited until midnight for work to be turned in. She had to reformat work and did not have all of the references. One part of the project was copied by a student and submitted without citing.

Hi Group,

It sounds like a lot of frustration here. In looking at your group discussions, enough time was given for all of you to submit your work in a timely manner, giving Jane plenty of time to put it together. Quite honestly, I think working past normal bedtime hours is commendable!

In the future, I hope that everyone gets his or her work in on time. Group projects are very difficult because you need to trust that everyone will do their share. Since a template for this project was provided, Jane should not have been responsible for putting the lesson plans in this correct format.

Furthermore, it is not up to one person to go in to find references, put lesson plans in the correct order, making sure information such as rubrics are not plagiarized. That really is not Jane's responsibility. That falls on the person who submitted the plagiarized work. We are all professionals here. We would not allow our students to get away with working in a group in this manner. We also would not allow our students to put down or talk harshly to each other.

I am sure some hard feelings have been created due to the aforementioned emails. I hope that you all can come together and make sure that amends and thank you's are made to the appropriate people for working so hard to help complete this assignment. Thank you, Jane, for all of your hard work. Thank you Jill for taking the time to reformat work submitted by others.

Scenario 3

At the beginning of an assignment, an email is sent to the instructor from a concerned student stating that the group is not coming together to make the necessary decisions to get the project started. Again, two different messages need to be sent: one to the student and one posted in the group area.

Hi _____,

I am so sorry that your group is having problems getting started. I will post a comment in your group area as well as send out an email to your group members that discusses dividing the unit.

Hi Group,

I took a peek in your group area to see how your group is coming along on your group project. I see you are having a little trouble getting started. Sometimes this is the most difficult part. Here is a suggestion that will help:

The unit topic that you have chosen to complete is called "All About Me". The grade level is kindergarten. Please choose which lesson plan you would like to do for this unit. Put your name beside the unit of your choice. Post this in the group discussion forum no later than Saturday night. If you have any questions, please do not hesitate to contact me.

Reading	*Science*
Math	*Art*
Writing	*Music*
Social Studies	*PE*

Sometimes group problems can be curtailed by being pro-active. The writers have had success in getting all group members to successfully work together by posting specific tips for group work. The following is an example.

This week you have your first collaborative assignment in this class. Working in groups can be extremely rewarding...or extremely frustrating. The collaborative assignments are just that – collaborative projects with the team held responsible for the final project in its entirety. Should your team choose to split up the project and one team member does not do his/her part, the team is still responsible for the final project in its entirety, which means the remaining team members may be graded down if there is an incomplete project. With that said, if a team member does not contribute at all or only in the most minimal way, he/she will not be eligible for a grade on the assignment, but his/her lack of participation will not be considered a valid reason for an incomplete assignment.

Working with groups online, without the benefit of face-to-face contact, adds another dimension to group work. In order to promote the most effective and successful collaborative experience, I have compiled these tips for success:

- *Provide alternate methods of communication (in addition to the course email and the discussion forums). Consider sharing alternate email addresses, instant messaging IDs, and/or phone numbers.*
- *Do your best to respond to all messages in a very timely manner.*
- *If you use Instant Messaging, post your IM chat logs on your discussion board. This allows anyone who missed all or part of an IM meeting to see what was discussed and provides a record of what was discussed. (Nonrelated discussion can be edited out.)*
- *Let your team members know of your preferred study schedule and any planned exceptions (e.g., Do you know you will be out of town for a few days? Are parent-teacher conferences coming up?).* **Have a plan** *for how to communicate emergency schedule exceptions.*
- *Review the collaborative assignments early. Establish roles for each project. (For example: Who will be the project manager? Who will do research? Who will compile the final document? Who will ensure timelines are met?) Determine whether these roles will stay the same for all collaborative assignments or will change.*
- *Establish each group member's responsibilities for each project and agree upon a timeline of due dates that works for everyone.*
- ***During collaborative assignment weeks, check into your team discussion forum every day.***
- *Remember your netiquette. Remain respectful at all times. Use emoticons and proofread your messages to make your messages are as you intend them to be. If you are frustrated, upset, or angry, you may want to wait before posting a message.*
- *Discuss conflict resolution before conflict occurs. How will you make decisions when there are dissenting opin-*

ions? How will you handle conflict in a timely and respectful manner? At what point would I need to become involved in a team conflict?

- *Before the designated group member submits the assignment for grading, each group member **must** review and okay the final assignment. This is each group member's responsibility.*

Another strategy that has yielded success is the use of a using a peer evaluation form. Post right away that each group member will complete the peer evaluation form for every member, including him or herself at the end of each group project. The instructor will use this information to assign the participation points of the project for each person. In most cases, the participation points constitute about 20 to 30% of the group project grade. Here is a sample peer evaluation form:

GROUP EVALUATION

COURSE _____ DATE ____/____/____

Please rate yourself and your group members using the following

Please rate yourself and your team members on the contributions that were made in preparing and submitting your group project. These ratings will not be shared with other members of your group.

In rating yourself and your peers, use a one to five point scale, where

USING THE SCALE BELOW, INDIVIDUALLY RATE EACH MEMBER OF YOUR GROUP, INCLUDING YOURSELF.

3= excellent   2=good   1=fair   0-poor

Insert your name in the first column followed by the rest of the members of your group in the remaining spaces.

NAMES					
PARTICIPATION					
ON TASK					
USEFUL IDEAS					
QUANTITY OF WORK DONE					
QUALITY OF WORK DONE					
TOTAL FOR EACH PERSON					

One of the largest problems is getting groups started. No one wants to jump in and be the leader of the group. The writers have taken time to read each of the assignments and look at different ways to divide the work into chunks for each member of the team to complete. In doing this, it is always important to leave one job of putting together the assignment and formatting to one person. Along with dividing up the work for the group, setting a timeline for completion helps the students to gage their time and get work into the group in a timely manner. Here are a couple of scenarios on how to divide the work for a group project:

Scenario 1:

This assignment will be completed by a group of four students. The assignment states:

Within your group, create a chart that shows the differences among students' learning styles; i.e. auditory, visual, and kinesthetic. Then outline the teaching approaches that address these differences.

Across the top of the chart, list the student differences, and down the left side, list teaching approaches that address those differences.

Since there are four students in this group, it will be very easy to divide this assignment between you. Please choose the assignment that you wish to do and place your name beside it no later than Tuesday. Post it to your group in this discussion thread. If you are not the first to respond, please read all of the discussion threads to see what has been taken so two of you are not working on the same part of the paper.

1. *student difference 1- kinesthetic learner*
2. *student difference 2- audio learner*
3. *student difference 3- visual learner*
4. *edit, format, and write final paper*

Here is a timeline for completion of your parts of the paper to make sure that the assignment is completed in a timely manner.

Thursday evening: *Individual work is submitted for compiling.*

Saturday morning: *Assignment is compiled, edited and formatted, and placed in group discussion forum for group approval or suggestions.*

Saturday evening: *Changes are completed on final paper and posted to discussion forum for approval of group.*

Sunday evening: *Final project is turned in by group members to assignments folder.*

Scenario 2:

This assignment is to look at different types of assessment. Place your name by the type of assessment that you would like to research. You will need to describe the assessments and how they are used. Then, analyze these instruments for reliability, validity, application, and content.

> *Criterion referenced*
> *Standardized*
> *Norm referenced*
> *Authentic assessments*

If you have a group of five, one person will be in charge of putting the paper together, editing, proofreading, formatting, etc. If you have a group of four, someone will need to volunteer to put the paper together and all of you will need to edit and proofread the work.

Here is a timeline for completing this assignment:

Tuesday: *Choose your assessment to research.*

Friday: *Turn in your portion of the work.*

Saturday: *Compiled copy is submitted to group discussion board for comments and editing.*

Sunday: *Final copy is posted for approval and then submitted for grading.*

Group activities can be one of the most difficult parts of facilitating an online course. Group activities take longer to complete than individual work because of the collaboration involved. Getting started early, organizing the assignment for the students, and making sure that assignment directions are explicit are essential to the success of any group activity.

Chapter Nine

Online Cheating

Mark Twain stated, "of all the animals, man is the only one that lies."

Student cheating in classes has been going on for a very long time. The issue of academic honesty and cheating is one that often is raised by skeptics of online learning. Whether or not cheating is more prevalent in the online classroom than the traditional classroom is uncertain, but it certainly is something that can and does occur. In the online forum, it is so easy to cheat. Instructors need to be diligent about watching for cheating.

Why do students cheat?

The question of course is why do students cheat? Some of the students are lazy. They do not want to take the time or make the effort to put together the paper on their own. It can be the easy way out. Some do not feel it is necessary for them to learn the material. Others are always in a rush to get things done. Even procrastination can lead to cheating. However, the main reason students cheat is because they simply do not know what constitutes cheating.

Many students have had cheating reinforced. Over the years of writing papers, they have taken information from sources, changed a few words using a thesaurus, and called it their own. They have put reference pages on their papers but never used citations. Perhaps they learned to use footnotes, but still paraphrase and copy sources.

As instructors, we need to make sure to clarify what is cheating. Cheating is to claim credit for the work of another person or using unauthorized materials or fabricated information in any academic work. This includes copying and pasting, changing a few words here and there, or not properly citing and referencing work used. It can also include "repurposing" a product from another class to submit for an assignment in a current class. It is important to understand what behaviors your institution considers cheating or plagiarism.

Identifying cheating

Identifying cheating on some papers is easy once you know what you are looking for. One of the easy identifiers are papers with different size fonts throughout the document or papers with intact hyperlinks. This is often caused by cutting and pasting from different documents. You may also notice the tone or language style changing between sections. Some students may try to insert their own ideas between copied sections to help the paper flow. Another one is having another students name on the title page! Or a paper posted for a course not yet taken in the degree program. Yes, it does happen. Any of these should certainly ring a caution bell.

You may also have the occurrence of a student posting papers way ahead of the due dates. The majority of the students work week to week unless they plan to be gone a week. They will most often notify you beforehand if they will be gone and ask about working ahead. One example of this is a student who posted a paper that had no bearing to the weekly assignment and started posting papers for other weeks in the course. Come to find out, this student had papers that were from a prior course before it was redesigned.

On the subtle side, it is much more difficult to detect some forms of cheating. It is so important to be active in the discussions. This will give you an idea of how the student writes. If the student's paper is totally out of sink from the way s/he has written in the discussions, it should make you question the integrity of the paper.

Paper mills do exist. Most of us have heard of them. When the author was looking for an editor to edit her dissertation, she was startled with how many hits she received on her search engine for dissertations for purchase. There is a plethora of papers for purchase on the Internet on any given subject. There are also places you can have someone else write a paper for a per page fee. Keeping in mind that most of the purchased materials will be broad in focus and, if the assignments are detailed, it may be difficult to buy a paper that fits the exact assignment. It is a good idea to let your students know that you are aware of the ability to purchase papers.

Educate the students

So, what can instructors do to make sure students do not cheat? First, including clear information and a firm policy regarding academic integrity in your syllabus lays the foundation at the onset of the class. It is important that you are familiar with your institution's policies and procedures regarding academic integrity and plagiarism so that your syllabus can reflect and support those.

Educating the student about what is considered cheating is the first thing an instructor should do. Instructors need to present materials about plagiarism: what it is, the correct ways to cite references from all sources including web sources. Setting up a special area for Tips is one way to do this. One title used is 'What in the world is plagiarism and what does it have to do with me'?

Below is an example placed into the classroom the first week of class.

Many students do not know the definition of plagiarism, aka academic dishonesty. Academic Dishonesty is defined as: "An intentional act of deception in which a student seeks to claim credit for the work or effort of another person or uses unauthorized materials or fabricated information in any academic work. Students are expected to be honest and ethical in their academic work. Academic dishonesty includes: cheating, fabrication, assisting, tampering, and plagiarism" (Oregon State University, 2004).

- *Cheating- use of unauthorized materials, information, or study aids. Unauthorized copying or collaboration on a test or assignment or using prohibited materials and texts.*

89

- *Fabrication- falsification or invention of any information including research, inventing or exaggerating data, and listing incorrect or non-existent references.*
- *Assisting- helping another commit an act of academic dishonesty. This includes paying or bribing someone to acquire a test or assignment, or taking a test/doing an assignment for someone else (or allowing someone to do these things for you).*
- *Tampering- altering or interfering with evaluation instruments and documents.*
- *Plagiarism- representing the words or ideas of another person as one's own or presenting someone else's words, ideas, or data as one's own. This includes copying another person's work (including unpublished material) without proper references, presenting someone else's opinions and theories as one's own, or working jointly on a project, then submitting it as one's own.* (Oregon State University, 2004)

With cutting and pasting, it is too easy to put together a paper using various websites and present it as your own work without referencing the sources. There are a several websites that sell graduate and undergraduate papers. There are also just as many websites to find out if there is plagiarism in your papers. Turning in a plagiarized paper can result in the end of your academic career. Even paraphrasing other sources can be picked up by search engines as well as websites utilized to find plagiarism. Even if you copy and paste a section of a website and then revise it to make it appear to be your own work, you must give the source that the information came from.

Ways to avoid Academic Dishonesty

Students who choose to learn online often do so because it fits into their already hectic lives. These students do not have the time to travel across town, find parking, and attend scheduled classes. Coupled with already busy lives, learners add the pressures of academia, which may cause many online learners to become over-

whelmed or pressured to complete assignments. This is when dishonesty can occur. The following strategies can help learners avoid unintentional academic dishonesty.

- *Do not procrastinate.*
- *Set aside enough time to do your best on assignments and study for tests.*
- *Include time to complete other activities for your family, yourself, and work.*
- *Find a tutor or form a study group to help in areas that are particularly difficult.*
- *Summarize sources you will use by making annotated bibliographies.*
- *If you use another person's words or ideas, you must give that person credit as the source.*

When writing a paper, you must do more than list every source in a bibliography. Even if you put the ideas into your own words, you will need to mention the authors, pages, and publication dates to show where your ideas came from. It is also good to back up facts with sources, otherwise they may look like opinion. If you use the author's exact words, enclose the words in quotation marks, or indent the passage if more than four lines. At the end of the quote, you must list the author's name and year of publication.

Some schools will give you some academic freedom to modify assignments. One tip is to add to the assignment asking them to add their personal experiences on the topic. Another strategy is to request alternate ways for students to present what they have learned, such as multimedia presentations, graphs or charts, etc.

Programs to help identify cheating

You will find some schools are affiliated with companies who review papers for plagiarism. One of these is called Safe Assignment. The instructor submits the paper and will receive back a document that tells how much of the paper is direct quotes and the sources that were quoted. Often you will see sources that are not even referenced in the student's paper. Or you will see the cited sources but no quotation marks have been used. Another area of Safe Assignment is where students can submit their own papers and receive results. Depending on your circumstances, you could require that all papers that are posted be submitted first and you require both the original document and a copy of the Safe Assignment report.

There are numerous detection programs available. Some of them are by subscription that the school purchases for students and faculty to use. There are some free ones on the Internet. The authors have also resorted to taking a phrase or sentence out of the paper and putting it into a search engine. This will often bring up papers that include the sentence. This is usually the first step in detecting a plagiarized source.

However, you do not need a commercial program to help you detect sources of plagiarized material. If you suspect a student's work may not be original, select a particularly unique passage and copy and paste it into an Internet search engine using quotation marks around the passage to keep it intact for the search. If the work is not original, often you will quickly be pointed to the online source of the information.

As instructors, we are not there to declare the students guilty before we have all the facts. However, when you discover that the student has cheated, you need to know what to do. Most universities have support; whether it is the department head, a mentor, or faculty specialists, you need to contact them to find out what you should do. Take the time to read the policies of your university.

Chapter Ten

Feedback and Grading

Donna was one of the best instructors I have ever had. She was very fair and provided excellent feedback with regard to our DQ postings and assignments. I look forward to having her again. The best instructor I have had in 15 classes.
David

Students need feedback on how they are progressing in all areas of the online classroom. Since this is a new way to learn for most students, it is imperative to give good feedback often. You will find that most schools have a set time that instructors are required to provide feedback on assignments. Some schools state that this feedback must be given within 48 hours while others give a full seven days. The authors have found that students appreciate timely feedback; usually within 48 hours. By providing feedback within 48 hours, it gives the students time to read the comments and make improvements on the next assignment. Waiting until the end of the next week to provide feedback on the students' work frustrates the students because they are unable to make any needed corrections before the next assignments are due. This can also frustrate the faculty member who must then grade another set of assignments with many of the same errors repeated. Giving prompt and specific feedback can alleviate many of these frustrations.

Rubrics are an important tool to use in grading and giving students feedback. Rubrics make grading more objective. It takes the "guesswork" out of grading student progress. Some schools provide rubrics for instructors to use while others expect the instructor to provide the grading guidelines.

Rubrics

Rubrics are quite time-consuming to make. The creation of a rubric is not only beneficial to the instructor but also to the students. It allows both to have more control over the outcome, since it is clear what criteria will be used to grade the assignment and students can determine what grade they want to work toward.

Below are rubrics used in all areas of the online classroom including participating in discussions, individual papers, group papers, and journals. You can modify the point distributions to meet your needs. In addition to these sample rubrics, you can find many rubrics on the World Wide Web that are available to you – just do an Internet search. There are also rubric generation tools such as Rubistar (www.rubistar4teachers.org) that may be useful to you.

Participation Rubic

	Exceeds expectations 20 points	Meets expectations 10 points	Working towards expectations 5 points	Does not Meet expectations 0 points
Responded to the assigned question				
Interacted with classmates about their responses to the discussion questions in a way which furthered discussion and critical thinking				
Actively engaged in classroom discussion by responding to a minimum of 3 peers				
Responses are professional, respectful, and collaborative				
Uses theory and practical application by incorporating personal examples, experiences or utilizing real-world examples				

Individual Assignments

	Paper Grading Rubric (based on a 10 point paper)			
Content	3	2	1	0
	Paper includes all requested components that have been thoughtfully and thoroughly examines; paper closely adheres to recommended word count guidelines.	Paper includes all requested components but may have been given only cursory examination; paper may be outside of recommended word count guidelines.	Paper includes some requested components; or only gives cursory examination; paper may be outside of recommended word count guidelines	Paper does not meet assignment purpose; paper is outside of recommended word count guidelines.
Organization	2	1.5	1	0
	Assignment is easy to read and follow.	Assignment is somewhat difficult to follow.	Assignment is significantly difficult to follow.	Assignment shows no evidence of organizational planning; paper rambles and is difficult to follow.

Individual Assignments - Continued

Paper Grading Rubric (based on a 10 point paper)				
Mechanics and Appearance	2	1.5	1	0
	Very minor or no mechanical errors are present	Few minor mechanical errors are present	Several mechanical errors are present)	The presence of many significant mechanical errors impedes comprehension of paper content;
APA Formatting	3	2	1	0
	All APA guidelines are followed; paper adheres to publication guidelines	Most APA guidelines are followed. 1-3 errors	Some APA guidelines are followed. More than 4 errors.	Did not follow APA guidelines
	APA citation information is correct (as applicable)			
Total				
Comments				

Group Assignments

Group Project

Paper Grading Rubric (based on a 10 point paper)

Content	3	2	1	0
	Paper includes all requested components that have been thoughtfully and thoroughly examined; paper closely adheres to recommended word count guidelines.	Paper includes all requested components but may have been given only cursory examination; paper may be outside of recommended word count guidelines.	Paper includes some requested components; or only gives cursory examination; paper may be outside of recommended word count guidelines	Paper does not meet assignment purpose; paper is outside of recommended word count guidelines.
Organization	**2**	**1.5**	**1**	**0**
	Assignment is easy to read and follow.	Assignment is somewhat difficult to follow.	Assignment is significantly difficult to follow.	Assignment shows no evidence of organizational planning; paper rambles and is difficult to follow.

Group Assignments - Continued

Group Project			
Paper Grading Rubric (based on a 10 point paper)			
Content			
3	2	1	0
Mechanics and Appearance			
2	1.5	1	0
Very minor or no mechanical errors are present; paper adheres to publication guidelines APA citation information is correct (as applicable)	Few minor mechanical errors are present; paper adheres to most publication few APA citation errors are present (as applicable)	Several mechanical errors are present; paper does not adhere to most publication guidelines in Welcome announcement; few APA citation errors are present (as applicable)	The presence of many significant mechanical errors impedes comprehension of paper content; paper does not adhere to most publication guidelines many APA citation errors are present
Participation in CLC			
3	2	1	0
Contributed substantially to CLC assignment. Met all group and class deadlines.	Contributed to the CLC assignment. May have needed reminders to turn in work on time to the group.	Contributed to the CLC but assignments were late.	Did not contribute to CLC assignment.
Total			
Comments			

Journals

	Yes	No
Student reflected on his/her learning from the reading, discussions, or assignments during the week. (5 points)		
Student included a personal reflection addressing how he/she will apply this new learning to his/her practice. (5 points)		
Total	
Comments	

Remember, when using rubrics, make sure to make them available to the students prior to using them for grading so students will know your expectations and how they will be graded. This should help students master your learning objectives by guiding their work in appropriate directions. When you have completed scoring the students' papers, return the rubric to the students. This saves time writing extensive comments. Instead, you can just highlight relevant segments of the rubric. Then add up the points for each section and add a section for comments at the end. It is also very important to give qualitative feedback along with the rubric to each student.

Making comments

Still, making comments on every student's paper can be tedious and time consuming. Often, it is difficult to come up with comments for everything. A great shortcut that the authors have utilized for several years is to create a comment sheet for each paper of a class. After you make the first comment sheet, you will only need to change the comments for the content section for additional papers.

One author likes to use the free Opera browser (www.opera.com) as a tool for making comments in the learning management system. Opera includes a notes bar where you can save and file text-based notes that can be clicked, dragged, and dropped into any Internet-based text field. The author has found this to be a great timesaving technique for making common comments. She will still personalize the comment appropriately, but being able to quickly drag the comment "template" into the text field has saved her lots of time.

Here is a comment sheet used for grading a paper:

Content

1. *Excellent job meeting the criteria for this paper. I really like the section that you wrote.....*
2. *Congratulations on an excellent paper!*
3. *Thank you for submitting an excellent paper! You have demonstrated that you have a clear understanding of the....*
4. *You have clearly identified....*
5. *You have effectively and fluently covered the points of the assignment in your paper.*
6. *You tackled an extremely interesting topic and made some very insightful observations. It is obvious to me that you critically analyzed the topic with in-depth research and came to solid conclusion.*
7. *The information in your paper was well written, and you did a great job of communicating it to the reader.*
8. *Thank you for submitting your paper. I found your section on .....was very good. However, I noticed that you did not mention the section of the assignment about .... Perhaps it was an oversight. One way to make sure that you do not overlook sections of an assignment is to copy and paste the directions onto your working copy. As you thoroughly address each section of the assignment, merely erase the directions. This will en-*

sure that all parts of the assignment are met. If you have any questions, please do not hesitate to ask.

9. *I am happy to assist you if you are having difficulties with the report on .... Let's discuss what we can do to help you complete this course successfully.*

Spelling and Grammar

1. *Your spelling and grammar is excellent!*
2. *Your paper is very difficult to comprehend because there are so many grammar, punctuation, and spelling mistakes.*
3. *I did notice that there are numerous errors in mechanics in your paper. Please proofread and or have others read your paper before submitting.*

4. *All papers turned in for grading should be of university level quality. Please read again the section of the Syllabus referring to Grammar and Punctuation.*
5. *It is so easy to become too close to your work and overlook simple errors. One thing that I have found works for me, is to read the paper aloud or to someone else. I always seem to find more errors that way. After you have read the attached edited paper, please let me know if I can be of further assistance.*

Style and Format

1. *Excellent references to back up your comments.*
2. *Regarding APA, the font used on all papers should be either 12-pt. Times Roman or 12-pt Courier. Please see p. 285 of your APA Manual for information regarding font.*
3. *The correct usage of APA with a personal conversation is found on section 3.102, p.214 in your APA Manual.*
4. *I have made some comments on your paper of some things that need to be addressed. The first one is a direct quote without quotation marks. Please see section 3-34 in your APA Manual for this information (p.117)*

Closing comments

1. *It is great to have you in our classroom and I am looking forward to your next paper. Keep up the great work.*
2. *Please continue to excel in your future classes; it has been a great pleasure to have you in my class.*
3. *I can tell you put a lot of time into your paper.*

Here are the step-by-step directions for making your comment sheet:

1. Open a new Word document,
2. Make a heading for each section of your rubric: content; grammar and spelling; and, style and format.
3. Make comments for each type of error a student makes in each area of the rubric.
4. Make comments for the students' strengths for each area of the rubric.

As you grade, cut and paste the proper comment onto the student's paper. You will find your grading time cuts down to almost half the time it was taking before.

Chapter Eleven

Working with Difficult Students

Anytime I had a problem, regardless of the nature of it, Danan was been there for me, cheering me on, supporting me, and guiding me. I appreciate her candor and strength. The online learning program is so much more challenging than the traditional graduate school setting. I never imagined the challenges it has presented! However, I am so thankful that I choose this path, as it has made me a better person. It has been through my online experiences with Danan's guidance that has been such a positive experience for me.

Leslie

This chapter will probably be the most frequently visited chapter in this book. In the years of teaching online, the authors have been presented with many challenging students. Students are very forward to instructors these days, and with the anonymity provided by the nature of online instruction, students are more likely to questions and challenge faculty members than they may otherwise be. Gone are the days when the instructor's word was the last word. Although problem students are rare, as online instructors you will need to be prepared for the student who challenges a grade, acts up in the classroom, the student with excuses, ones who plagiarize, or even those who disappear for a period of time and come back expecting you to grade all of the papers.

Discussions

As instructors, we will all be challenged by a difficult student at least once in our careers. These situations can be difficult to address and even harder to prepare for because we do not know what situations will arise. It takes a skilled instructor to be able to stop problems that do arise either in the face-to-face classroom or online.

Problems in the online classroom can be intensified because they are there for everyone to see. It is not like the face-to-face classroom when the discussion can be changed and the poorly said comment all but forgotten. In the online discussion forum, comments are written and posted in haste by students eager to share their ideas and perspectives. Often the students do not stop and consider the tone or meaning of their words before sharing the response with the class.

The majority of our students are busy with careers, families, and other activities. Add to that a fast-paced online course with weekly assignment deadlines, challenging subject matter, an enormous amount of reading, and working virtually in small groups. The stress can be tremendous which may contribute to the occasional outburst of frustration or not taking the time to really look at what is written prior to posting.

We are all guilty of sending an occasional email or making a statement we later regret. This is truly understandable but not an excuse. Being empathetic does not mean we ignore the student's tone or inappropriate communication. However, we need to make sure that we do not aggravate the situation by using a confrontational tone with them.

Instead, address the problem in a professional manner with the idea of using it as an opportunity for growth and enrichment. Often, once the student goes back and rereads the posting, we see a second post that says "Oops! This did not come across the way I intended. I tried to delete it but it will not let me. I am so sorry. What I meant to say was…." This type of response shows that the student is not only reading his/her messages, but also reading it from the perspective of the other students. Usually this type of incident requires no response to the student.

The best way to promote positive interactions is to be proactive. In the expectations for the course, conduct for communication should be stated. These expectations should also refer the students to the school's code of conduct. The second way would be to model appropriate communication in our classes. Being actively involved in discussions is the most effective prevention of difficult situations by our students.

Below are some guidelines to keep in mind as you address challenging students in your classes:

1. Stop. Often times in a situation where you are dealing with a difficult student or situation, you become angry or flustered. One thing great about online teaching is you can walk away, collect our thoughts, and take the time to word your communication carefully. Never respond to a student when angry or upset as the words may come across in that tone.

2. Remain Professional. When you respond to the student, stay professional no matter how inappropriate the student becomes. Add a section into your communication that shows that you care about the student and want the student to be successful. This can help to defuse the situation. Do not cause your own conduct to come into question.

3. Praise in public; correct in private. If a student makes an inappropriate comment in class, redirect the comment in a positive manner. Often this will be all that you need to do to stop the problem. If this message does not stop the discussion, send a private e-mail that states the university's code of conduct and inquire how you can help the student be successful in the discussions.

4. Seek assistance. When in doubt, ask your university for help. There is someone at your university whether it is a mentor, department head, or faculty specialist that is there to help when problems arise. Get their phone numbers and emails and keep them available to you at all times.

5. Do not ignore student-to-student disagreements. Your classroom is your responsibility. To disagree calmly is one thing, but to begin an argument is another. All students are expected to adhere to the university's code of conduct. If a student conflict erupts, you must address it immediately.

As the instructor of the class, you play an important role in guiding discussions to make sure students stay on track. That is why it is so important to monitor the discussions on a daily basis and provide both general and specific feedback along with positive reinforcement for particularly good contributions.

Even with monitoring the discussions and giving feedback, it does not mean that problems will not arise. Please remember that it is never appropriate to correct a student in front of the class. A good motto to follow is to "praise in public and correct in private." The proper place to provide correction is through private emails between the instructor and the individual student. This creates a log of the discussion if problems occur again or continues. The writers caution about using the telephone as it leaves no evidence that the conversation took place. However, if using the phone seems to be the best alternative to stopping the problem, following up the conversation with an email recapping the telephone conversation, will create a log.

It is important to post something in the classroom so all students can see that the problem is being addressed. If a private email is the only follow-up, then the other students may feel that the problem is being ignored and not feel safe to freely express themselves in the classroom. It is very important to build a sense of community in which the students feel safe to take risks. By not addressing this problem, the classroom community can be ruined.

In the classroom post:

Hello Class,

I would like to start off by thanking the class for the participa-

tion in the group discussion. The discussions have been quite lively and thought provoking. With that in mind, I would also like to remind you that not everyone has the same beliefs, ideas, or points of views. This is the beauty of having a group discussion. Everyone is able to share their thoughts and opinions with each other and have people respond to them. People will agree on some things and disagree on others and that is ok. It becomes a problem when someone personally attacks another for the simple reason that they disagree with their beliefs or ideas. Let us remember that we all come from different backgrounds and experiences in life and we should be able to share this with others without the worry of being attacked. Once again, I would like to say that the class has done an excellent job of participating and I look forward to more lively discussions. If you have any further questions please refer to the student and handbook and, as always, feel free to contact me.

Take care,

A private email would also be sent to the learner.

Dear Student,

This past week you wrote a message in our discussion board that had a "sour" tone to it and I just wanted to take the time to remind you that it is important to reread your work before you post it. Unfortunately, when we write responses to the discussion board, the people reading them lose valuable communication tools because they do not have the opportunity to see or hear the people writing them. Therefore, the words must stand for themselves.

In the case, of last week, your message came across harsh towards the other student. I just wanted to check-in with you and make sure that you are O.K., or is something going on in your life that would cause you to send this type of message? Maybe this was just a fluke and the words in this message came across harsher than what you had intended? Either way, I need to hear back from you, as I am concerned.

As you know, it is important that we celebrate in other's diversity and learn from them so that together we can share our knowledge. We have the opportunity here to make a difference in this world, and we do not want to turn our backs on anyone or any ideas. The more we share, the stronger our knowledge becomes.

Please let me know what is going on in your life and how I can help you.

Thank you,

Both writers have experienced problems in the classroom that needed to be addressed in private. The first incident is a student who writes an insulting comment to the instructor in the discussion forum. If this happens and it is possible, remove the comment from the forum. Then send the student a private email.

I am not sure if you are aware of the tone of your post in the discussion forum. Perhaps I have taken it the wrong way but it appears to be insulting. While I appreciate comments and concerns from students but I expect them to be professional and nonbiased without racial or demeaning comments.

These will not be tolerated in the classrooms, assignments, journals, or in emails. I have removed the offensive post in the discussion forum. Please refer to the student handbook for proper netiquette in the classroom. If there are any more comments posted with this tone, I will be forced to take university action.

Another problem that may arise is a discussion that becomes out of control. This is the reason why universities want instructors to be active in the discussions. If an instructor is active in the discussion, usually s/he can see a discussion going the wrong way and turn it around. However, there are times when a discussion can become out of hand very quickly. Again, the class needs to know that you are addressing the problem. Therefore, a note needs to go into the classroom that reminds them of proper netiquette. Then a note needs to go to the student involved in the heated discussion.

110

I noticed that the discussion about celebrating holidays was getting a little heated. Please remember that everyone is entitled to their opinion. If you do not like their opinion, please choose to abstain from the discussion. I have redirected the discussion to concerns about parents and other students taking offense to the celebrations and how you would handle this.

Please, if you have a concern about another posting, please email me or call me rather than responding in negative ways. We need to keep our discussions positive. If you have any concerns, please do not hesitate to contact me.

Another problem that may arise in the classroom is the student who responds to everyone. Some students may feel that it is necessary to read every post and respond. This causes a high amount of stress for as you know it takes hours to read all of the discussions posted in a single week. In this event, it is really easy to help the student with some suggestions.

Hi,

I just wanted to tell you how much I have enjoyed reading your responses in the discussions this week. It is so easy to get caught up in them. I did notice that you have responded to every person in the class. This takes a lot of time and is not necessary. The requirement for responding to others is three responses per week.

What I found that helped me when I was an online learner was to choose four or five students to read the initial postings each week. I could vary this to read different students each week. Then I would respond to three of them. I found I was getting just as much out of the discussions and was not becoming stressed for time.

Please contact me if you have questions or concerns about my suggestions. Again, let me assure you that your contributions are great and I look forward to reading more of your postings.

The other problem with a student who responds to everyone can be stifling the discussions. The one student takes over the discussions as the authority on the subject, which causes the rest of the students' participation to be lowered. Again, a private email to the student can be very helpful.

Hi,

Thank you for sharing your wealth of knowledge about our topic this week. I am impressed with your ability to respond to each student's posts with an appropriate antidote or example. However, your quick responses may stifle the creative thinking of other students in our class with less experience in this area.

Could you help to help the other students by limiting your responses? I do not want to lose your great contributions, but I do want to stimulate the thinking of all the other students as well. Instead of responding to all postings, could you pick out the 4-5 threads to participate in; leaving the others to the rest of the class?

Please contact me if you have questions or concerns about my suggestions. Again, let me assure you that your contributions are great - we just need to have better participation from some of the other students.

Management Problems

Students used to respect their instructors. They would never question a grade, let alone tell the instructor that the grade was too harsh and they want it changed. Today, this happens quite a bit. If we give in to what the students want, then we are putting the integrity of the program on the line. We need to be careful with grading papers to make sure that there is minimal error. Make sure directions for the assignments are clearly written. Then use a rubric to make sure grades are objective. Make sure that feedback is explicit to the rubric.

Another problem that you will often have to deal with is the student who makes excuses. Some instructors have a no excuses policy. The authors believe that "life happens." A student may become ill, there is a family emergency, or this particularly week at work had more demands than usual. These are all viable excuses and students may ask for extensions on their due dates for papers. The problem arises when this becomes habitual or the student waits until the last minute to ask for an extension.

Students who fall behind the first week in class will tend to fall behind the entire class. It is the snowball effect. Be careful in accepting excuses from the same person more than twice a course. Let the student know that this is the second time that s/he has asked for an extension and it will be the last time it is granted.

The other problem is students who wait until the evening the assignment is due and ask for an extension. In one class, Danan had seven students ask for an extension on an assignment within four hours of the cut-off time. Believe me; students know that they need extra time the day before or even earlier in the week. It is best to set a policy that an extension needs to be asked for a day in advance or it will not be granted except for extenuating circumstances such as the Internet went down or the electricity went out.

I know that life happens. It does with me too. Please take down my phone number (123) 456-7890 and save it in your telephone. Please take my email dmyerswylie@cox.net and save it in your address book on your computer. That way you can get in touch with me if there is an emergency. I am very understanding about problems and will gladly give you more time when necessary to finish an assignment as long as you ask me a day in advance.

It is easy to take advantage of a kind-hearted instructor. With the pace of these classes, being late one week can create a snowball effect. Please be aware that a maximum of two extensions will be given per term.

Late assignments will be accepted for a maximum of 7 days. NO EXCEPTIONS!!! I will not give credit for any assignments turned in after that time. This means assignments that you have gotten permission to turn in late or not.

Occasionally a student will disappear for a week or two. In large classes, it is easy to lose track of students in the discussions and not notice their disappearance until the end of the week. In addition, some students will wait until the last day to pop into the classroom and complete all assignments. A little email checking on the student may help you to find out if the student is experiencing a problem with the class or life itself.

Oops! Did the assignment box drop your paper? Did it disappear into cyberspace?

With your track record of diligence in the class, I am concerned that your assignment that was due last Friday was not submitted. As you know, this project represents one-fourth of the grade you will receive for this course.

Please contact me and let me know how I can help you. I am happy to work with you so you can successfully complete this assignment and the class.

- or -

Are you O.K.? Last week's assignment is missing from our inbox and you have been so good with turning in all of your other assignments, which made me very concerned. I see that you are doing a very nice job in our discussion room and so I wanted to reach out to you and see what happened. Please let me know how I can help.

Correcting Papers

By far, the hardest problem to handle is plagiarism. Sometimes students actually plagiarize out of ignorance. For years, students have been able to take information and paraphrase or change a word here and there and call it their own. It has become a habit that has been ingrained since elementary school. A few things can be done to educate the person who plagiarizes out of ignorance.

1. Begin the course by having a plagiarism policy stated in the syllabus and welcome announcement to the class.
2. Define plagiarism and give explicit examples.
3. Give the students resources on proper citations and referencing.
4. Post a sample paper that uses proper APA format and style.
5. Set a class policy for handling plagiarism and stick to it.

Posting these items does not mean that students will not plagiarize. As stated in the chapter on plagiarism, there are websites available that you can turn a paper in if you suspect plagiarism. A report will be written that shows the plagiarized material and the sites in which it was copied. The best thing to do is make this report available to the student. Stick to the facts in your response to them.

We agreed at the beginning of the course to format all papers in the APA Style that allows students to make correct in-text citations. The Syllabus states clearly that "I expect you to use APA in-text citation, reference format and paper set-up parameters. APA style should be applied to references, proper margins, consistent font type and size, title page, heading level, page numbering, spacing, and other elements. You will find significant deductions for lack of adherence to APA style."

Correct APA citations add clarity, improve structure, and, most importantly, give you the right to claim authorship for your findings and give the deserved credit to other sources. Academic honesty is highly valued. Let me remind you that words or ideas that require citations include, but are not limited to, all hard copy or electronic publications, whether copyrighted or not, and all verbal or visual communication when the content of such communication clearly originates from an identifiable source.

I trust you will avoid such unintentional omissions in future research. Please let me know if your need further clarifications.

Sometimes the student really did not plagiarize. The sources are listed in the reference section correctly but citations are not used. This is a time to educate the student.

Thank you for submitting your paper, which I can see you have some excellent resources listed, which adds depth to your paper.

One thing I would like to draw to your attention to is your failure of citing your sources properly. Please refer to the APA information posted for you in the classroom for help with citing your sources. You can also refer to the student handbook or student learning center of the university for extra help in your writing style.

You may also run across the student who really tries to format a paper correctly but does not have sources referenced or cited correctly. Again, this can be used as a learning experience.

I have just finished grading your first paper for this course, and I want to commend you on the great job you demonstrated with your research. You obviously have a true passion for your work, and it shows through the many examples you provide throughout your report. One area where you might want to focus on next time is on your references. You have some inconsistencies and errors with your citations. You might want to review the current APA guidelines. Log on to http://www.apastyle.org/previoustips.html for answers to some common APA questions. Refer to the classroom information on APA Tips or refer to your APA Manual. Overall, your paper was good. With some careful attention to these details, you will maximize your points for your next assignment. If you have question, or if I can be of help in any way, please let me know.

The instructor must stay highly involved in the classroom to curtail any problems that may arise. We want students to express their opinions but not at the expense of others. Likewise, an instructor needs to know the policies set by the school in which s/he works and make sure that the students are aware of the guidelines for participation, academic honesty, and being successful in your courses.

References

American Psychological Association (2001). *Publication manual of the American Psychological Association* (5th ed). Washington DC: American Psychological Association.

Conrad, R.M. & Donaldson, J.A. (2004). *Engaging the online learner: Activities and resources for creative instruction.* San Francisco: Jossey-Bass, Inc.

Friedman, A., Joseph, D., Schubart, J., Sheridan, D., & Wyatt, T. (2002). Online learn: Designing online debates. Retrieved on June 7, 2004 from http://onlinelearn.edschool.virginia.edu/debate/predebate.html

Gibbs, J. (1994). *Tribes: A new way of learning together.* Santa Rosa: Center Source Publications.

Griffis, A. (2007). APA tips sheet. Write Well, Write Now, Inc. www.wwwnUSA.com

Ip, A. I. (2004). Online role playing. Retrieved on June 8, 2004, from http://adulted.about.com/cs/technology/a/onlineroleplay.htm.

Newman, D.R. (2003). Project learning logs and reflective reviews. Retrieved on June 8, 2004 from http://www.qub.ac.uk/schools/QueensUniversityManagementSchool/Education/ModuleOutlines/MISOutlines/Filetoupload,56761,en.pdf.

Oregon State University (2004). Academic issues. Retrieved on May 31,2004 from http://oregonstate.edu/admin/stucon/achon.htm#achon.

Palloff, R.M. & Pratt, K. (1999). *Building learning communities in cyberspace: Effective strategies for the online classroom.* San Francisco: Jossey-Bass, Inc.

Palloff, R.M. & Pratt, K. (2001). *Lessons from the cyberspace classroom: The realities of online teaching.* San Francisco: Jossey-Bass, Inc.

Palloff, R.M. & Pratt, K. (2003). *The virtual student: A profile and guide to working with online learners.* San Francisco: Jossey-Bass, Inc.

Piaget, J. (1969). The mechanisms of perception. London: Routledge & Kegan Paul. *Publication Manual of the American Psychological Association*, 5th ed., 2001.

Vygotsky, L.S. (1981). The genesis of higher mental functions. In J.V. Wertsch (Ed.), *The concepts of activity in Soviet psychology.* Armonk, NY: Sharpe.

Wines, J., & Bianchi, J. (n.d.). Online teaching and learning: Faculty reflections. Retrieved on June 7, 2004 from http://www.2002.org/CDROM/poster/179.